THE JANE AUSTEN RULES

Also by Sinéad Murphy

Effective History:
On Critical Practice Under Historical Conditions

The Art Kettle

THE

Jane Austen
RULES

A CLASSIC GUIDE
TO MODERN LOVE

SINÉAD MURPHY

MELVILLE HOUSE UK
LONDON

THE JANE AUSTEN RULES

First published in 2014 by
Melville House UK
8 Blackstock Mews
Islington
London N4 2BT

mhpbooks.com   facebook.com/mhpbooks   @melvillehouse

This paperback edition published in October 2014
The right of Sinéad Murphy to be identified as the author of this work
has been asserted by her in accordance with the Copyright,
Design and Patents Act of 1988

A CIP catalogue record for this book is
available from the British Library

ISBN: 978-0-9928765-1-7

1 3 5 7 9 10 8 6 4 2

Design by Christopher King

Printed in Great Britain by Clays Ltd, St Ives plc

To my mother, Joan, whose love of literature meant
that I read Jane Austen when I was still very young

CONTENTS

The Real Thing   3

Reader, *Marry Him*!   127

THE JANE AUSTEN RULES

'After all, there is no enjoyment like reading!'

THE REAL THING

It *ought to be* a truth universally acknowledged, that a young woman in possession of a large number of modern dating guides must be in want of Jane Austen! Why? Because the novels of Jane Austen are still our *safest* guide to the rough-and-tumble course that is true love. The aim of this book is to prove that this is so.

But can Jane Austen's novels *really* offer advice that our bestselling dating books cannot? What, after all, can they really have to tell us, that we have not now been told at least a hundred times over? – That women have substance to them, that is what! That women are *the real thing*.

When Jane Austen began to publish, around the beginning of the nineteenth century, novels were not yet all that popular. Young ladies instead passed their time by reading *conduct books*, Regency England's equivalent of the modern dating guide, full of dos and don'ts for the woman who wished to flourish in

society. Gradually, however, women began to spend less and less time reading conduct books and more and more time reading novels, which also provided advice on what a woman should and should not do, but in a manner that was much more entertaining and – very importantly! – much more *emancipatory*.

You see, the Regency conduct book tended to judge a woman by how she conducts herself – that is, by how she *acts*, by how she *seems*. The novel, by contrast, was concerned with what women are *really* like, admitting – perhaps for the very first time – that women too have a fulsome interior life, with thoughts and feelings that are as crucial to get right as the actions that follow from them. In the novel it was much more important that a woman cultivate herself than that she learn how to *appear* to do so, much more crucial that she be truly worthy than that she learn how to make herself *seem* so. In the novel, in other words, women were allowed to be *real*, and not merely the cardboard cut-outs to whom the conduct book directed its advice.

And Jane Austen was at the forefront of it all, presenting to the Regency world a host of real women – so determined to do so, indeed, that she invented her very own narrative style, which gives the reader almost unrestricted access to the internal life of her female characters. The Regency conduct book stood very little chance, once Jane Austen's women of flesh-and-blood began to appear on the scene!

In the light of which, ought it not to be all but impossible that the conduct book would once again become women's literature of choice? What an idea! – that we might turn a second time to a genre that holds our sex in such contempt. And yet, we have done it – our bestseller lists are clogged these days with dating guides that revive the terrible premise: that women have *really* nothing about them, and must resort to rules of *conduct* to have any chance of love.

'Don't you have somewhere to go or something to do? Or can you pretend you do?' ask the authors of one of these bestselling guides. 'You want to seem like you are interested in politics, sports, and the world in general, not just guys!' But why must women merely *seem* like they are interested in politics, sports and the world in general? Are they not really so?! Not according to the modern dating guide, which, like its Regency conduct book ancestor, has little, if any, faith in women and so would spend our energies on *seeming*.

One evening, in the drawing room at Netherfield Hall, *Pride and Prejudice*'s Caroline Bingley – clearly an avid reader of the Regency conduct book! – holds forth on what it is for a woman to be 'accomplished.' Her list of requirements is a long one – it extends so far as to demand 'a certain something' in the tone of a woman's voice! – but it is solely concerned with the project of *seeming*, of a woman's *appearing* to have something of interest about her.

Miss Bingley is quickly corrected by Mr Darcy, who reveals his true regard for the female sex by insisting that a *really* accomplished woman must 'add something more substantial, in the improvement of her mind by extensive reading.' But just look at how blinkered is Miss Bingley's response: the very next evening, she is found with a book in her hand, it is true, but a book she has chosen only because it is the second volume of the book Mr Darcy has chosen! Her attention, we are told is 'quite as much engaged in watching Mr Darcy's progress through *his* book, as in reading her own,' and, though she loudly declares to the company, that 'after all there is no enjoyment like reading,' she follows this statement by yawning and throwing her book aside, 'quite exhausted by the attempt to be amused with it'! Miss Bingley, you see, is a woman who thinks only of *conduct*, and is therefore incapable of the 'something more substantial' which Mr Darcy so justly demands.

'Don't you have somewhere to go or something to do? Or can you pretend you do?' – such is the guidance offered by the authors of *The Rules*. They might as well have said, 'Don't you have something to read? Or can you pretend you do?' – for, the modern dating guide, just like Caroline Bingley, is wholly dedicated to *seeming*. It is enough that a woman strike a pose, enough that a woman play a part, enough that a woman act as if, enough that a woman *conduct herself.*

But if this does not suffice to make us loathe the very notion of conduct, if we find ourselves now and then still browsing in the conduct section of our nearest bookstore, then we might as well consider this: devoting ourselves to seeming may not succeed even on its own terms! The subtitle of *The Rules* prom-ises to reveal secrets for 'capturing the heart of Mr Right,' but Caroline Bingley, for all her efforts to seem like a reader in the drawing room at Nether-field Hall, fails to capture the heart of Mr Darcy – 'She could not win him,' we are told. And why not? Because men, in general, want more than mere *conduct.* Men, in general, want more than cardboard cut-outs. Men, in general, desire the real thing!

Think, then, of how fortunate we modern women are, to have the novels of Jane Austen to turn to once again! – so that we might rediscover what our Regency sisters learned for the very first time: that *real* women really do have somewhere to go and something to do, that *real* women really are interested in politics, sports and the world in general, that *real* women really do read books – in short, that *real* women are *the real thing*!

* * *

Jane Austen did share *something* with the conduct book: she too believed we could do with a little guidance now and then, especially in the complex matter of love. The idea of our having a few simple rules was not, therefore, one to which she objected. But there are two different kinds of rules: there are rules for conduct and there are rules for *character*; there are rules for seeming and there are rules for *really being*. There are rules, in other words, and there are *Jane Austen* rules. And only the second are worth our following.

Two hundred years ago, Jane Austen's novels triumphed over the conduct book, on the strength of her conviction that women are *the real thing*. Let *us* only rise to that very same conviction, and her novels are sure to triumph once again.

Do we not know that we ought to be too heavy for
even a grown-up man to carry?

BE A WOMAN,
NOT A *GIRL*

'Be a Creature Unlike Any Other' is the very first rule of that bestselling guide, *The Rules*. It is a rallying cry, for self-expression and -realization. It is, however, sadly misconceived, rank with the kind of rivalry that has beleaguered us women for centuries. In 1949, the French thinker Simone de Beauvoir wrote that women have been and still are 'the second sex' because of their reluctance to say '*we* women,' their wont to isolate themselves from other women, to regard other women as competition. Already with their very first rule, then, the *Rules* authors would place us women in an age-old human trap, which, by dividing us, works to conquer us.

One evening, again in the drawing room at Netherfield, Miss Bingley observes that 'Elizabeth Bennet is one of those young ladies who seek to recommend themselves to the other sex by undervaluing their own. But it is,' she concludes, 'a paltry device.' Miss Bingley, of course, is employing the device herself at this moment, seeking to recommend herself to Mr Darcy by undervaluing the merits of Elizabeth.

But she is right, at least in this: looking to promote oneself at the expense of other women, setting oneself up as a creature unlike any other, is a paltry device, and one that has kept us women 'in our place' for as much of time as history can recall.

But there is worse. De Beauvoir imagined our biggest problem to be our reluctance to say 'we.' She little knew how far we had yet to fall. For, now it seems our biggest problem is our reluctance even to say 'women'! *The Rules* addresses its advice almost invariably to 'the girl,' construing its reader as not only jealous of other members of her sex, but hardly herself a fully paid-up member! When it comes to that paltry device, of seeking to recommend ourselves to the opposite sex by undervaluing our own sex, there is surely nothing more paltry than this refusal even to admit that it *is* our own sex! Of course, it is a serious hindrance to women's fight for equality, if we do not seek solidarity with our kind; but it is a worse hindrance again, if we do not even identify with our kind!

Jane Austen might seem a surprising precursor for the likes of Simone de Beauvoir, and yet the first Jane Austen rule is right up de Beauvoir's alley: be a woman, not a girl, it advises, and make the very best you can of your biological and cultural destiny; be a woman, not a girl, it commands, and give yourself at least a fighting chance of improving on that dreaded second place!

Persuasion is the novel above all others in which this Jane Austen precept is set down, pitting the froth-and-foam attractions of the *girl* against the so-much-more-substantial merits of the *woman*. It is not quite pistols at dawn, but it might as well be! It is after breakfast, on the Cobb at Lyme: Louisa Musgrove makes a foolish leap and lies crumpled and unconscious on the ground, while Anne Elliot, Louisa's rival for the love of Captain Wentworth, remains strong and unscathed, undisputed mistress of the scene. Anne does not stand over her opponent in victory, admittedly, rather bending over her in womanly concern, against a backdrop of foam breaking harmlessly over the granite of the pier. But it is a victory nonetheless, as Louisa makes a quiet exit from the novel, and a revived and blooming Anne assumes first place, at centre stage.

Anne Elliot is twenty-seven years old at the opening of *Persuasion*, twenty-eight at its close. She is the oldest of Jane Austen's heroines by a considerable distance, and would have been judged by the standards of her time as well and truly departed from girlhood. 'A few years before,' the opening chapter tells us, 'Anne Elliot *had been* a very pretty girl.' Those years are gone. But it is this, it turns out, that is her greatest strength. For, compared with the womanly fortitude of Anne Elliot, the ephemeral claims of Louisa Musgrove will always leave *her* an 'also ran.'

Louisa Musgrove's flirtation with Captain Wentworth consists of little more than jumping over stiles and off steps so that he might catch her in his arms as a father does his child. Little wonder the female sex persists in being the second sex, if this is the way its members tend to behave! And it is. For, Louisa Musgrove's childish overtures towards Captain Wentworth capture precisely the mode of relation into which books like *The Rules* would place us all, as they impart to us a myriad of tricks and schemes to provoke our man into being what is thought manly – rendering should-be women into grotesquely strapping schoolgirls, cramming tips on how to squeeze into a gymslip! Cannot we see that we look incongruous in this pre-pubescent guise? Do not we know that we *ought* to be too heavy for even a grown-up man to carry? There are, of course, very different roles to which the sexes are assigned in our society. And there is often little merit in refusing them. But to *force* them, as Louisa does, to seek always to heighten their effect, is not only unnecessary, it is undignified. And, worst of all, it keeps us women from being womanly, by preoccupying us with ensuring that men are manly!

The fact is, we women ought to be far less anxious than *The Rules* book and its like would have us be. For the fact is, a good man will be manly pretty much of his own accord. He will help us over stiles and guide us down steps, and do a million more essential manly things, without our ever having to pressure him to do so. Indeed, if we pressure him to do so, and if, having made him do so, we pressure him to do so again and again, he will, in the end, let us down. Compare Louisa Musgrove's childish lurchings with Anne Elliot's quiet, independent progress on the walk to Hayters' farm, making her way carefully and on her own, and becoming the object of Captain Wentworth's care and concern when he observes her fatigue *for himself* and takes decisive, careful action to relieve it. Who can forget that moment when, *unsolicited by Anne*, he places his hands gently but firmly around her waist and assists her into Admiral Croft's gig, to be driven the rest of the journey home? How much more affecting, how much more romantic, how much more *sustainable*, this, than all the girlish leapings and fatherly catchings in the world! And that is but the beginning of Captain Wentworth's self-originating manliness, for he arrives very quickly at a point at which he must and does exert all his energies to secure Anne Elliot's *un*outstretched hand.

It is true, of course, that the *girls* in Jane Austen's novels do many of them find love in some shape or form. For, girls are most of them pleasant enough – Louisa Musgrove, for one, is described as an 'amiable, sweet-tempered girl.' (This, as it happens, would make her a perfect candidate for *The Rules*, which advises that, on the first three dates, we be 'sweet and light' and 'like a summer breeze.') But girls lack punch, to use a pithy kind of phrase, and are good for little else than *seconding* a man. Behind every great man is a great woman, so the saying goes. But it does not go right. For, *behind* any kind of man – in that unseen, unheard, supporting role – can only ever be a *girl*.

A sweeping glance at the litany of Jane Austen's girls suffices to prove this painful point: Lucy Steele of *Sense and Sensibility* is nothing more than a means of relieving the boredom of Edward who, when he finally meets a woman in Elinor, bitterly regrets his early engagement and desires nothing but to escape from it; Maria Bertram of *Mansfield Park* is but Henry Crawford's instrument for revenging Fanny's refusal of him, and is tossed aside when she is no longer useful; Isabella Thorpe of *Northanger Abbey* is merely the excuse for Captain Tilney's sowing his wild oats, and is abandoned without security or prospect when the Captain has moved on to someone else; foolish Lydia of *Pride and Prejudice* is a last-minute impulse of Mr Wickham, who requires to flee his debtors and thinks that he might as well bring a willing young companion along with him for distraction; and poor hapless Harriet is paid compliments by the ambitious Mr Elton only as a stepping stone to Emma Woodhouse, whose hand in marriage is really his first object.

And what of Jane Austen's poster-girl? What of Louisa Musgrove, who in the end marries the estimable Captain Benwick? All in the novel are surprised at this outcome. Is it our one counterexample to the second-class status of the girl? It is not. For, the only plausible explanation for the match is that Benwick requires a substitute, to console him for the loss of his wife, Fanny Harville, and will content himself with the first one who (literally!) falls at his feet. Louisa will never be more than second best in Captain Benwick's heart, for a woman, even a dead woman!, will always trump a girl.

Louisa and Henrietta Musgrove are described when first we meet them, as 'like thousands of other young ladies, living to be fashionable and merry.' And that just about sums them up: two girls among a thousand girls; two girls in a job lot; two girls whom no one will recall. Admiral Croft declares himself defeated by the effort to distinguish them –'I hardly know one from the other!' he cries. And even Captain Wentworth seems confused, it being unclear for most of the novel which of them he is actually courting! And when the Admiral begins to inform Anne of Louisa's engagement to Captain Benwick, he has first to be reminded of Louisa's name. 'I wish young ladies had not such a number of fine christian names,' he complains. 'I should never be out, if they were all Sophys, or something of that sort.' What the Admiral really wishes, of course, is that young ladies did not so completely disappear into a mass of girls in which it is impossible to distinguish them, but comported themselves more like Sophy, his sensible, well-informed, *womanly* wife.

Towards the close of *Persuasion*, Captain Wentworth reflects on the eight long years since he and Anne first fell in love. 'It is a period, indeed!' he says. 'Eight years and a half is a period.' And it is – by far the longest test of constancy to which Jane Austen subjects any of her characters. And all in pursuit of the very simple point: that a *woman* is well worth the remembering. A girl, by contrast, is eminently forgettable, and for a really quite obvious reason – Everybody knows that Neil Armstrong was the first man to walk on the moon ... but do many remember Buzz Aldrin, the second man to do so? Edmund Hilary will go down in the annals as the first man to the summit of Mount Everest ... but will any recall Sherpa Tanza, the second man to reach it? When should-be women are content to live as girls, they can never escape their fate as the second sex, and the second sex, like the second everything, will always be forgotten.

In the delicious early days of their reconcilement, Captain Wentworth assures his Anne that that eight-and-a-half-year period, between their first and second engagements, is as nothing – 'To my eye,' he declares, 'you could never alter.' Naturally, we must allow something here for the partial blindness to which any true love consigns us. Anne certainly does, reflecting, with some amusement, that 'it is something for a woman to be assured, in her eight-and-twentieth year, that she has not lost one charm of earlier youth'! Yet, there is no denying the truth in the Captain's compliment. For, it was the *woman* in Anne he had always admired, and women, like all who come in first, are not to be diminished by months or by years. Mere girls may have a limited shelf life, but women, like the wine with which they are often coupled, are only ever improved by the passage of time.

Simone de Beauvoir wisely saw that women are held back by not saying 'we.' But Jane Austen saw something even more fundamental: that women are held back by not saying 'women.' Then, let us, this instant, determine to be *women*! Let us hold up our heads and speak with assurance, as Lizzy does with Darcy during that awkward first dance at Netherfield Hall. Let us have conviction and live by it, as Elinor does when she promotes the fortunes of Edward so that he might more easily marry his foolish Lucy. Let us, like Emma, have opinions and not be afraid to air them. Let us, like Marianne, have ideals and not be afraid to pursue them. Let us, like Catherine, be intrigued by the world and alive to its wonders. Let us, like Fanny, be serious and composed and as steadfast as can be. And let the words of Captain Wentworth be as truly said of us as they are of Anne: 'A man does not recover from devotion to the heart of such a *woman*! – He ought not – he does not.'

We are not children, *reaching wilfully*
for the thing that looks *the sweetest.*

FIND A MAN,
NOT A *GUY*

'Most men are content to sit around in a recliner on a Saturday afternoon and drink beer and watch football.' So say the authors of *The Rules*. And their advice? 'Take up a hobby,' presumably so you have something to do while he is thus otherwise engaged. But Jane Austen's advice is somewhat different: when confronted with the scene just described, do not find yourself a hobby; rather, find yourself a *man*! There is nothing inherently objectionable about recliners, beer, football, or Saturday afternoons, of course; many a couple may *together* enjoy any combination of these delights as often as they choose. But when a man is content to enjoy them on his own, and with such a degree of indifference to you as to consign you to the desperate measure of taking up a hobby, then that man is not a man but, to use a favourite *Rules* word, a *guy*. And there are at least as many reasons for not dating a *guy* as there are for not being a *girl*.

Freud had a theory about boys, in which boys are so envious of their father that all they can think of is overthrowing him, by the simple means of killing him and marrying their mother. A somewhat bloody scenario, it is true, but (so long as it remains fantasy!) a natural phase in the progression of boys into men – according to Freud at least. But some boys just get stuck, and spend their whole life in defiance of father-figures and desirous of mother-figures. These boys never grow into men. Instead, they grow into *guys*.

Naturally, the term 'guy' was not abroad in Jane Austen's time, but we need not much concern ourselves with that. For, the condition it describes was almost as common then as it is now. Jane Austen's novels are full of *guys*, and, much more relevant to this volume, of the women they would make into their *mothers*.

Perhaps Jane Austen's most perfect example of a *guy* is Mr Frank Churchill, that charmed creature who wreaks such havoc in the little village of Highbury in which the novel *Emma* is set. He is introduced to the reader of *Emma*, as he is to the residents of Highbury, well before he makes an appearance in the flesh, a visit from him so long anticipated by his father, Mr Weston, that his failure to make it is a topic for discussion among all in the village. He is talked of as coming, but does not come; he promises to come, but does not come; he makes arrangements to come, but does not come; he is expected to come, but does not come. Even Emma, who is inclined to be rather taken with the idea of Frank Churchill, admits that 'he ought to come,' that 'one cannot comprehend a young *man*'s being under such restraint, as not to be able to spend a week with his father, if he likes it.'

And Emma has touched upon the truth: for, Frank Churchill does *not* like it, but likes only to give rise to the anticipation of it, so that poor Mr Weston might be driven to greater and greater lengths in finding lame excuses for his son. If ever there was a way to kill your father, slowly and by a thousand cuts, then this is it. The fact that Frank Churchill has long ago relinquished his father's name in favour of the name of his adoptive mother proves the point conclusively: here is what Freud would call a case of the Oedipus Complex; here is what Jane Austen would call a 'coxcomb,' a 'puppy,' a 'trifling and silly fellow'; here is what we would call a *guy*.

And who is the woman so ill-advised as to have involved herself with this guy? Miss Jane Fairfax, as disapproving yet forgiving as ever a devoted *mother* could have been. She is neglected by Frank, toyed with by Frank, made witness to Frank's follies and the butt of Frank's jokes; she is forced, time and again, to discipline Frank, by exhortation and by example: but still she stands by him, loyal and loving to the end. She feels the burden of having found a *guy*, certainly, being prone to such low spirits that she seems likely, at one point, to break down entirely. This is explained at the time, by her having very soon to enter upon the life of a governess in order to earn her living. But, as we discover at the novel's close, Jane Fairfax was never in danger of having to become a governess, being all along secretly betrothed to Frank Churchill. Then, why the low spirits? Why the melancholic focus on the trials of being a governess? Why such despair, at a fate she knows she will never have to face? Because it is a fate she knows she *will* have to face, destined as she is for a lifetime's ministrations to a *guy* who might as well be a very unruly child!

During one highly charged scene in the novel, Jane Fairfax likens the governess-trade to the slave-trade; they are 'widely different certainly as to the guilt of those who carry it on,' she admits, 'but as to the greater misery of the victims, I do not know where it lies.' Poor Jane Fairfax!: confronted with a future in which she will have to combine the corrective vigilance of the governess with the unalloyed devotion of the slave; a future, that is, in which she will have to be a mother to her *guy*.

Then why does Jane Fairfax stick with him? Why does she not simply leave her *guy*? She clearly suffers from the relationship, and intermittently shows signs of wanting to end it. Why, then, does she not do it? It is a mystery, indeed. Until, that is, you ask yourself this: about how many women might we wonder the same, women who are troubled by their relationship, exploited in their relationship, exhausted with their relationship, but nonetheless stick with their relationship? The mystery about Jane Fairfax, it turns out, is the most common-place mystery of them all, and explained by this single simple fact: that it is not easy, in fact it is sometimes impossible, to say goodbye! to a *guy*.

Given which difficulty, it behoves us to be very careful of never saying hi! to a guy – hence the second Jane Austen rule. How curious, then, that one has to wait for the *twenty*-second rule in the second *edition* of *The Rules* for a similar warning, for a single chapter devoted to the idea that there is such a thing as Mr *Wrong*. And even then, *The Rules* concludes by observing that one woman's Mr Wrong 'is another woman's Mr Right'! For all that is to be said about women, it seems, *The Rules* has little definitive to say on the topic of men.

Why this lack of consideration, we may ask, of a matter that is nearly the most pressing of all? Why this lack of urgency, this *laissez-faire*? The answer lies not so very far away: in the title of the chapter in question, in which the type of man one ought to avoid is described as a 'buyer beware.'

We are accustomed nowadays to thinking of almost everything as a commodity, to be bought and sold on the market. We buy an education, a home, child care, even youth!, so why not think in terms of buying a *guy*? But there is at least one reason why not, and it is this: no matter how expensive a purchase we make, we are always more prepared to cash in that purchase than we are for cashing in a *guy*. Because a *guy*, for all his faults, is still human, and can therefore inspire feelings of attachment that a mere commodity never can. It is a category mistake by the authors of *The Rules*, to imagine for a moment that it is as if we are buying a *guy*. And it is a costly mistake too, for, though you may sell your house and trade in your car, you may never be able to make an exchange on your *guy*! NEXT! shouts *The Rules*, when a man proves himself to be less than he seemed he might be. But a mere NEXT! will not, and ought not, suffice to be rid of a fellow human being. Better take the whole thing much more seriously, then, and devote a *second* rule, not a *twenty-second* rule, to finding a man and not a *guy*.

And there is an even greater urgency to this issue when we realize that *guys* are often packaged rather invitingly. Not awkward and taciturn like Mr Darcy, not tired and disappointed like Colonel Brandon, not serious and devout like Edmund Bertram nor caustic and superior like Henry Tilney, not ordinary and modest like Edward Ferrars nor old-fashioned and brusque like Mr Knightley nor weather-beaten and strident like Captain Wentworth, *guys* are smooth-talking like Mr Wickham, groomed and at ease like Henry Crawford, dashing and impetuous like Mr Willoughby, good humoured and care-free like our very own Frank Churchill. But, though charm and good looks, smooth talk and good humour, may be all very well at first, they do little in the end to sweeten the man for whom you must always play mother.

But what does all of this matter?, you may ask. Will it count for anything when our eyes meet across a crowded room? When thunder sounds and lightning strikes? When our heart misses a beat? 'You can't always help who you fall in love with,' as *The Rules* points out. Stuff and nonsense!, comes Jane Austen's reply. We should *meet* a man, not *fall* for one! None of Jane Austen's heroines *falls* in love. Elizabeth positively dislikes Mr Darcy at first; Marianne considers Colonel Brandon too old for romance; Emma looks upon Mr Knightley as a kind of uncle, Fanny upon Edmund as a much-loved brother; Elinor likes Edward but in a manner that strikes the romantic Marianne as insipid; Anne, though she may have fallen in love at nineteen, certainly does nothing so foolish at twenty-eight; and Catherine is so caught up in the fallings in love of the heroines of her favourite novels that she forgets altogether about doing the same herself and gives her hand to Henry Tilney in appropriately calm and collected style.

But there is wincing; there are sighs: such an *unromantic* account of romance! Then, why have Jane Austen's novels been read with such persistence for over two-hundred years? Why have the tales she told left us with some of our most enduring romantic pairs? Because romance is best served with a dollop of *reason*: that is why. Not too much, of course, or the main dish is somewhat dry. Charlotte Lucas's decision to marry the odious Mr Collins, on the principle that enough of love will follow *after* they are married, is one to send a shudder down every woman's spine, including her author's. But Charlotte, by her own admission, 'is not romantic, you know.' We, by contrast, are. But we are not *children*, reaching wilfully for the thing that *looks* the sweetest. We are rational beings, as well as romantic ones. We have the right to choose. We should exercise it.

It is sometimes said of a woman, that she will 'make a man of him.' Even Mr Knightley seems to think it possible, during the heady first days of his own engagement to Emma, declaring himself ready to believe that Frank Churchill's character 'will improve, and acquire from Jane Fairfax's the steadiness and delicacy of principle that it wants.' Do not believe it, Mr Knightley! Lydia will not make a man of her Wickham, nor Miss Grey of her Willoughby, nor even Jane Fairfax of her smiling Frank Churchill. Boys may very well grow into men, but *guys* never ever do!

*But must we really listen to the likes of Mrs Bennet and
Mrs Jennings, in all their incessant triviality?!*

RULE 3

LISTEN TO
WHAT THEY SAY

Pride and Prejudice begins with one of the most famous lines in English literature: 'It is a truth universally acknowledged, that a young man in possession of a large fortune must be in want of a wife.' The line is intended ironically, of course. That the earth orbits the sun is a truth universally acknowledged; that a young man in possession of a large fortune must be in want of a wife is no more than *what they say*. And yet, *is* the young man with a large fortune, in this case, in want of a wife? Indeed, he is. Mr Charles Bingley, young, rich and (a bonus!) handsome, sets his sights on Jane Bennet almost as soon as he sets foot in the neighbourhood. That a young man in possession of a large fortune must be in want of a wife is, in this case at least, a truth as worthy of universal acknowledgment as that the earth goes round and round the sun. It seems that *they* know a thing or two after all!

Given which, it may be surprising that *they* include Mrs Bennet, a woman whose merits do not comprise any wonderful intellectual acuity. Yet Mrs Bennet is *Pride and Prejudice*'s great champion of the truth about young men with large fortunes, and is shown thereby to possess a kind of *wisdom* which her well-educated husband is utterly without. Oh, Mr Bennet is clever enough to make great sport of his wife, declaring at one point that he hesitates to send Mrs Bennet to visit Mr Bingley on the grounds that his universally acknowledged want of a wife might lead Mr Bingley to make an offer to Mrs Bennet herself! – Very amusing, to be sure. But, for all his wit, Mr Bennet has none of that common sense with which his wife is equipped and which he regards as foolish to the extent that he regards it at all.

In the end, of course, it is Mr Bennet who is found to be foolish, for not paying heed to *what they say*, when they say that a young man in possession of a large fortune must be in want of a wife, a truth that Mr Bennet ought indeed to have acknowledged with enthusiasm, on account of his having never bothered to make the kind of financial provision for his wife and daughters that might have made young men with large fortunes a matter of indifference to them all.

If there is one thing remarkable about Mr Bennet, it is that he seems always to have his head stuck in a book, always to be found in his library, from which hallowed ground the Bennet females are, for the most part, banished. The nuggets of wisdom that *they say*, then, are clearly not to be derived from the study of books. Indeed, insofar as *they* include Mrs Bennet – a woman, we can presume, who has never opened a volume in her life! – it is certain that *what they say* is to be learned by some means other than by reading. More than this – that burying your head in a book might rather prevent you from hearing *what they say* than anything else! For, *what they say* is to be gleaned simply by opening your ears, and listening out for those truths that bear repeating, time and again.

The Rules describes its rules as 'time-tested secrets for capturing the heart of Mr Right.' But here is a contradiction in the very title of their publication. For, *time-tested* rules are never secret; they are rather universally acknowledged. In fact, whether or not they continue to be universally acknowledged, whether or not they continue to bear repeating, is the very test to which time subjects them. In other words, if a rule has stood the test of time, it has done so not by being the kind of thing *they hide*, but rather by being the kind of thing *they say*.

To demonstrate, we need go no further than the biggest 'secret' to which *The Rules* claims to give us access: the 'secret' that a woman should be mysterious. Consider, if you will, all of the ways in which this so-called 'secret' has been and continues to be the kind of thing *they say*: 'Treat him mean and keep him keen'; 'Keep him guessing'; 'Hold something back'; 'Tender yourself more dearly'; 'Through a chink too wide there comes in no wonder,' and so on and so on, to such endless length that the notion that the mysterious rule is a 'secret' is made to seem utterly ridiculous. Secrets? Time-tested rules, the kind of things *they say*, are rather the sound-track to our lives, broadcast in stereo and often somewhat louder than we would wish for!

Certainly louder than Marianne Dashwood would wish for, as she struggles to drown out the sound of *what they say*, during her ill-advised courtship with Mr Willoughby. One day, having gone unaccompanied with Willoughby, to look around the house he expects to inherit, she is cautioned by her sister Elinor, who informs her of what she cannot herself be unaware of: that *they say* her behaviour is bound not to come to any good. 'My dear Marianne,' urges Elinor wisely, 'as it has already exposed you to some very impertinent remarks, do you not now begin to doubt the discretion of your own conduct?' 'If the impertinent remarks of Mrs Jennings are to be the proof of impropriety in conduct, we are all offending every moment of our lives,' is Marianne's defiant reply. 'I value not her censure any more than I should do her commendation.' Foolish Marianne! The censure and commendation of Mrs Jennings are precisely what she should value, founded, as they are, upon that brand of wisdom that has withstood the test of time.

But must we really listen to the likes of Mrs Bennet and Mrs Jennings, in all their incessant triviality?! Indeed we must, says Jane Austen, and be glad to do so too! We have learnt to look down upon the particular concerns of such women, of course, being nowadays so very modern, so very urbane. But it is precisely the particularity of their concerns that gives Mrs Bennet and Mrs Jennings that intimacy with time-tested truths which all the libraries in the world are not able to furnish. For, their field of study is human nature, and there is no better way to learn of human nature than by thinking *and talking* of human beings. Mrs Bennet and Mrs Jennings are none other than the 'chatterbox mother' and 'gossipy next-door neighbour' of which *The Rules* speaks so dismissively – but, though *The Rules'* authors tell us that a man does not wish to *date* them (What of that? Mrs Bennet and Mrs Jennings would neither of them dream of dating anyone!), Jane Austen tells us that a woman should certainly wish to *heed* them.

You see, not everything worth knowing is to be found between the covers of books; and not everything worth listening to is to be heard from the mouths of those who read them. On the contrary, there is a kind of knowledge that is to be had only by virtue of the 'chatter' and 'gossip' at which Mrs

Bennet and Mrs Jennings are so adept. And, in the end, even the superior and studious Mr Bennet is forced to admit it. Having refused to pay heed to Elizabeth's warning, that her sister Lydia's wild behaviour is giving rise to the censure of 'the world,' Mr Bennet must come at last to accept that neither the censure nor the commendation of 'the world' is to be taken lightly but is to be listened to as a pretty reliable guide in human affairs, which, if followed, would in this case have prevented the disgrace of Lydia's elopement and the sacrifice of a young girl's future. Remorseful, if only for a time, Mr Bennet compliments Elizabeth on having shown a 'greatness of mind' of which he had not been capable. And that is it in a nutshell: women – especially women as inquiring and impertinent as Mrs Bennet and Mrs Jennings – tend to have the 'greatness of mind' that comes not from reading but from 'chatter,' not from study but from 'gossip'; it is certainly worth listening to *what they say*.

Are *books* like *The Rules* utterly redundant, then? Ought we to put them down entirely, and stride forth in search of the nearest Mrs Jennings? Are novels themselves to be abandoned! – offering, as they do, those insights into human nature that a Mrs Bennet might give us in the merest half an hour? Not necessarily. There can be no harm, after all, in transcribing *what they say*, much less in animating and illustrating *what they say* in the manner achieved so brilliantly by Jane Austen. Moreover, given that the conditions for 'chatter' and 'gossip' are on the wane in modern life, it may be that, far from there being harm in it, there is great good in the recording and publishing of *what they say*. But we ought to be clear that we are doing no more than that: no more than recording and publishing what are well-known, well-worn rules, no more than repeating once again what are universally acknowledged truths. One recent edition of *The Rules* calls itself *Not Your Mother's Rules*. But, if there is anything between its covers that is of use or of value, then it can only be because the 'secrets' it 'reveals' in fact *are* your mother's rules: just the kind of thing that your mother, or my mother, or Mrs Bennet, or Mrs Jennings would advise; in short, just the kind of thing *they say*.

It is to be expected, of course, that *they* will sometimes get it wrong. Perhaps nobody knows this better than poor Anne Elliot, who, by the time we meet her, has already sacrificed eight years of happiness on account of having listened to *what they say*. *They say* that a young man *not* in possession of *any* fortune must *wait* for a wife until he can earn a decent living, and so nineteen-year-old Anne relinquished her engagement to the penniless Captain Wentworth. How bitterly Anne regretted having listened to *what they say*, we can only imagine, as, within two short years, *she* lost her bloom while *he* won his fortune. All we are told is how loudly she now feels she could speak out, in favour of the 'cheerful confidence' of youth and against the 'over-anxious caution' of the world. What Anne Elliot learned the hard way is that you should *listen to* what they say, not necessarily *do* what they say.

But that is not all that Anne Elliot learns. For, late in the novel, she discovers that she would not, after all, speak out quite so loudly against the 'over-anxious caution' of the world. It is late one morning, in the Musgroves' lodgings in Bath. Mrs Musgrove and Mrs Croft are talking together 'just in that inconvenient tone of voice,' we are told, 'which was perfectly audible while it pretended to be a whisper.' It might be Mrs Bennet and Mrs Jennings in the room, for all the 'chatter' and the 'gossip' that Anne is forced to hear! But just then, from the clamour of 'undesirable particulars,' emerges a nugget of the wisdom that no philosophical treatise would easily afford. The topic is the upcoming nuptials of Henrietta Musgrove and Charles Hayter:

'And so,' says Mrs Musgrove, 'we thought they had better marry at once, and make the best of it. At any rate, it will be better than a long engagement.'

'That is precisely what I was going to observe,' replies Mrs Croft, 'I would rather have young people settle on a small income at once than be involved in a long engagement.'

'Oh! dear Mrs Croft!' cries Mrs Musgrove, 'there is nothing I so abominate for young people as a long engagement.'

'Yes, dear ma'am,' returns Mrs Croft, 'or an uncertain engagement, an engagement which may be long.'

And so on and so on go Mrs Musgrove and Mrs Croft, continuing 'to re-urge the same admitted truths.'

But Anne has heard enough, enough to realize that when *they say* that a young man *not* in possession of *any* fortune must *wait* for a wife until he can earn a decent living, then *they* ought not to be simply disregarded. For, *as they also say*, there is nothing worse than the kind of long and uncertain engagement that Anne was most likely set to endure had she not broken with Captain Wentworth when she did. Anne Elliot is a great enthusiast for reading, but only by overhearing 'admitted truths,' bandied about in audible whispers between Mrs Musgrove and Mrs Croft, does she learn that her eight lonely years were not entered into unwisely.

Anne hears nothing further of the conversation on long engagements. Not very distinctly, at least. 'It was,' as we are told, 'only a buzz of words in her ear.' But how important the *buzz* of Mrs Musgrove and Mrs Croft! How crucial the *chatter* of Mrs Bennet and Mrs Jennings! How essential this chorus of women, with its 'inconvenient tone' and its 'undesirable particulars,' giving us insights into life and love that are to be had from nowhere else! How great indeed, *what they say*!

It is a truth universally acknowledged that the course of true love never did run smooth. If so, it is a course on which you need all of the help you can get. Then do not defy 'the world' without a thought. Do not close your ears to *what they say*.

Women are not uni-form, but multi-form . . .

RULE 4

DRESS UP

The fact is, there are no rules for dress. Not even for dressing for love. Oh, many more books than *The Rules* would attempt to detail such rules, selling us secrets on how to 'dress for men,' extolling the virtues of such garments as push-up bras, short skirts and high heels. But, it will not do. These books would persuade us that there is a uniform for love, but the notion is fatally flawed. For, women are not uni-form, but multi-form; and, though *one* form of woman – tall, slim, fair and outgoing – might be flattered by short skirts and high heels, most forms of woman would end up perfect frights. A push-up bra on a *flat-chested* woman? Incongruous! A short skirt on a *middle-aged* woman? Undignified! High heels on a *tall* woman? Just plain dangerous!

And at any rate, men, for whom these publications would have us dress, would hardly notice if we dressed in a sackcloth! When *Northanger*'s Mrs Allen asks of Henry Tilney, whether that gentleman 'understands muslins,' he replies that he does so particularly well – 'I always buy my own cravats,' he says, 'and am allowed to be an excellent judge;

and my sister has often trusted me in the choice of a gown.' Mrs Allen, we are told, is 'quite struck by his genius,' and observes with some degree of feeling: 'Men commonly take so little notice of those things. I can never get Mr Allen to know one of my gowns from another.' But Henry Tilney, as is his wont, is merely humouring Mrs Allen, and, like almost all of his sex, does *not* 'understand muslins' – or silks or sashes or ribbons or bows or any other of the aspects of women's attire. Mrs Allen might as well have held on to the knowledge with which she began: men, in the main, commonly take very little notice of how we dress.

The notion that we ought to dress for men is, then, a foolish notion indeed. And we ought to dispense with the rules for how to do it, rules that would reduce us women to a second childhood, during which we dress in the morning in what was laid out for us on the night before. In fact, we ought to dispense with the rules of 'fashion' more generally, for they are founded on this misguided premise: that women, *grown women!*, are unable to dress themselves.

In Jane Austen's time, the fashion was for what is called *empire line*: fitted sleeves and bust, with skirts falling directly downward from just beneath. It was a style well suited to an active and elegant life, being without the corsets and crinolines with which Victorian times so risked women's comfort and safety. But it had more to recommend it even than this. For, it was a fashion influenced by the Regency enthusiasm for all things *Classical*, which was then thought of as the guarantee of *timeless* beauty and *eternal* truth; the straight fall of the empire line, without hoop or voluminous undergarment, was Regency England's revival of ancient Greek attire. We might say, then, that the fashion of Regency England was to avoid being merely fashionable, to strive for something much more, well, *classic*. And, though modern women, very rightly, may judge not to follow this fashion in its *particulars* – the empire line does little to enhance a narrow form, for example – we all of us ought to emulate its *essentials*: by seeking to be other than merely fashionable; by judging how best to make our particular form into something beautiful and true; in short, by dressing ourselves.

And what could be more natural than that adult women should dress themselves? Yet, we seem, these days, not to know how to do it!, remaining for the most part in a state of *un*dress, our bodies (barely!) covered in what is called 'causal clothing,' lauded for its infamously easy accommodation of form and of movement. Why should anyone bother to 'understand muslins' now, when all we need do is don a second skin, when we can be in the world as we are in our living room, when all the rage is for *dressing down*?

But Jane Austen can tell us why we should still

bother to 'understand muslins' and their like. Regency England had little of the formality of the Victorian Age, when even the legs of the piano were dressed up!, but the requirement that we put on something more than a second skin – something other than 'leggings' and a 'vest top' – would, at any time since the garden of Eden!, hardly count as a formality at all, just a basic condition of civilized existence. The world, after all, is not our living room. Oh, it may feel comfortable, natural even, to lounge about as if it were. But Adam and Eve took their Fall precisely for acting as if the world were their living room! And ever since, it has been part of what it means to be human, not simply that we cover ourselves but that we *clothe* ourselves, not simply that we throw on whatever's easiest but that we *dress up*, deliberately and with care.

On second thoughts, then, perhaps there is, after all, one rule for dress. It has been an unwritten rule for all of human history, but may now require to be recorded. And it is this: *clothe* yourself; *dress up*!

When Mr Bingley, on the morning of that happy day when at last he proposes to the forbearing Jane Bennet, arrives so early that the Bennet ladies are 'none of them dressed,' what is it that happens next? Does Jane leap up, and with careless ease saunter downstairs in her stockings and shift? Do the rest follow fast upon, hastily donning their Regency second skins, as so many Eves to Mr Bingley's Adam? Of course not! Though Mr Bingley may not know one gown from another, he would certainly have known had there been no gowns at all! As it is, however, Jane delays long enough to perfect even such details as the sash on her gown. And Mrs Bennet too gets dressed up, for all her eagerness to secure the young man with the large fortune, waiting so patiently downstairs.

We might object, of course, that there is great *freedom* to be had, by just throwing on some 'sweats' and hanging out. But we had better consider this: that there are false freedoms as well as true ones – that 'sweats,' in short, may not really be as liberating as they feel.

It is unlikely that many of us will have the chance to try on, say, one of those little Regency coats with which Jane Austen's heroines encountered the weather, but those who will are promised a wholly *uplifting* experience: shoulders wider, back straighter, and head higher than ever before. Why this? Because Regency clothing did not, for the most part, stretch, and so imposed on its wearers a much more careful pose, a much more regulated movement, a much more dignified bearing, than we are now accustomed to achieve – the little Jane Austen coat, carefully tailored, gives the idea of dressing *up* an entirely more vital significance! Which would be cold comfort, of course, were this elevating effect to be had only from clothing of the Regency age. But it is not. Our nearest vintage clothes shop is stocked full of garments that will do the business just as well: dresses and skirts, trousers and jackets, which, because they do not stretch much, lift us up like never before.

In the end, throwing on some 'sweats' only seems to promise freedom; for, by stretching to fit all our shapes and sizes, casual clothing has made us slumped and shuffling, not exactly on all-fours, it is true, but somewhere there or thereabouts! Freedom? On the contrary! *Dressing down* has so rounded our shoulders and bent our heads, so curved our spines and knocked our knees that we are the slaves to its fashions in a horribly almost-literal sense! It turns out that if you can kill a man with kindness, you can shackle a woman with ease. And we need not even throw on some 'sweats' nowadays to fall victim – even when we get 'dressed up' we are likely to find ourselves in something so stretchy, we could probably compete for the pole vault in it, if the unlikely occasion arose!

In these oh-so-liberal times, *constraint*, of movement or of attitude, is anathema. But some constraints can make us free, just as some freedoms can make us slaves. Jane Austen's heroines' attire is described, when described at all, as being simply and beautifully fit – when Fanny Price is dressed for Sir Thomas's ball, her author remarks only on 'the neatness and propriety of her dress' – as if anything more or less would imply looseness of mind and of morals. Rather puritanical!, we might think. And yet there is no denying that there is something in it: when we straighten our spines, we think more clearly; when we regulate our movements, we feel more in command; when we hold our heads up high, well, we hold our heads up high! Perhaps a well-fitting dress does not secure everything of importance, but it is certainly ennobling, of body *and* of mind.

By Jane Austen's time, a 'muslin' referred not only to a certain kind of fabric, but also to those mock-up muslin gowns made by dressmakers to ensure a perfect fit, before the final article was sewn in a fabric more expensive. Indeed, the word 'muslin' came gradually to refer to any such mock-up gown, even when muslin was no longer used in their manufacture. Why should we bother to 'understand muslins'?, you ask. Because *the perfect fit*, with which the muslin came to be synonymous, is the key to that uprightness of bearing and of thinking that is, these days, in terribly short supply.

But if, after all of this, our concern is *still* to dress for men, we might as well pay some heed to this: though men may take very little notice of the details of our dress, though they may not know one of our gowns from another, they too are susceptible to the elevating effect of a woman who follows the golden rule, *dress up*. One evening, in the drawing room at Netherfield Hall, Miss Bingley names among the attributes of an accomplished woman, the possession of 'a certain something in her air and manner of walking.' Miss Bingley is not a character from whom we expect to hear much worth listening to, and yet when, on another evening, she takes a turn about the room and invites Elizabeth to do so too, Mr Darcy refuses her invitation to join them, partly on the grounds that he can admire their figures much better from his seat by the fire. Mr Darcy is teasing, of course. But would he have found Elizabeth quite so irresistible, would he have had later that evening to make a mental note not to pay her too much attention, had she slumped, slouched and stretched her way about the room? Mr Darcy may not know one of Lizzy's gowns from another, but he is not insensitive to the effect of a gown that *fits*: to that 'certain something' in Elizabeth's 'air and manner of walking' that he cannot help but find 'bewitching'!

Independence of mind, *not independence of means.*

RULE 5

BE *QUITE* INDEPENDENT

Emma's Mrs Elton, in her first encounter with the novel's heroine, declares her own suitability for the married state to be guaranteed by the fact that she is 'quite independent.' And she is, in a way, quite correct, having brought to her union with Highbury's vicar, a dowry of no less than ten thousand pounds. But it is another kind of resource than the pecuniary of which Mrs Elton boasts to Emma, the kind of resource that lies, as she puts it, 'within myself'; it is independence of *mind*, not independence of means, to which Mrs Elton, in this instance, would lay claim. And with very little justification, her head being full of nothing more than intrusions on the business of others and suspicions of being slighted herself. Still, Mrs Elton has the sense to know a golden rule if she has not the sense to follow it, and has her author's full support in this opinion if in no other: a woman's suitability for love is guaranteed when she is quite independent of mind.

All rather straightforward, we might think – these days, at any rate, in which women are as free as men to cultivate their minds. But there's a catch. Consult the Oxford English Dictionary on the definition of 'quite,' and discover that it can mean: either, 'to the greatest extent; *completely*'; or, 'to a certain extent; *moderately.*' So, though we might all these days agree that a woman should be quite independent, there is still the question of whether a woman should be completely independent, or only moderately so. Indeed, for women in the Western world, there is now no question of greater urgency. And Jane Austen has the answer, if we care to seek it out.

Contrary to the popular idea that she did little more than pen pretty pictures to amuse the status quo, Jane Austen contributed more than her share to the battle for women's independence. Politics was not her sphere, it is true; novels were. But in her novels, she made women's independence one of her very central themes. So much so, indeed, that the novel *Emma* works as a kind of morality tale, to show what we ought to mean when we say that a woman should be *quite* independent. The tale has its knight in shining armour – Mr Knightley, who else! – and follows the fortunes of three women, who, each in their turn, are considered as deserving to be his wife. And in the usual style of such tales, the first woman is discovered to be not independent enough, the second to be too independent, and the third, at last!, to be just – *moderately* – right.

When Harriet Smith makes a bid for Mr Knightley's affections, she is considered by Emma as not without a chance of securing them. But Emma is wildly mistaken. Harriet is never likely to attract the novel's hero, who simply observes: 'She knows nothing.'

Harriet Smith does know *something*, of course; she knows that she wants to meet a man. Taken on its own, however, this piece of knowledge does not result in a woman of any independence! On the contrary, so committed is Harriet to her one, single idea – the idea of meeting a man – she has no thought to spare for anything else, not even for the kind of man she wants to meet, much less for the kind of woman she wants to be! Any man will do for Harriet, so much so that her affections are subject to a series of substitutions, of Mr Elton for Robert Martin, of Frank Churchill for Mr Elton, of Mr Knightley for Frank Churchill, and, at last, of Robert Martin for Mr Knightley! Harriet ends right back where she started, but one has the keen sense that it would have made little difference to her had she ended with an Elton, a Churchill, or a Knightley instead, so long as she ended with someone.

As for having any thought for what kind of a woman she wants to be, Harriet is so bereft of ideas on this topic, so utterly indifferent to it, that she surprises even Emma herself by how quickly and completely she adopts her patron's views. 'What shall I do? What shall I say? Dear Miss Woodhouse, do advise me!' is Harriet's constant refrain. She is a woman quite astonishingly without independence of mind, her thoughts held wholly hostage by the idea of simply finding a man.

And Harriet does find a man – a man of character and respectability at that. Yet, all the world knows that her union with Robert Martin is nothing much more than a lucky break. 'The advantage of the match,' as Mr Knightley says to Emma, is 'all on her side,' and he predicts 'a general cry-out upon her extreme good luck.' This is unlikely to upset Harriet, of course – women who do not bother with independence of mind may often live happily every after. But the Jane Austen woman is not content with mere happiness. The Jane Austen woman demands also the dignity of finding love without losing self-respect!

The moral of Harriet's story, then, is that a woman should have at least some independence of mind. For, as Mr Knightley puts it, 'Men of sense do not want silly wives'!

Perhaps, then, it is the educated and accomplished Jane Fairfax who is to succeed to Mr Knightley's hand? She is certainly considered a likely candidate, Mrs Weston confiding to Emma at one point that she thinks it a very promising match. But it is not to be, not, as in Harriet's case, because Jane is too little independent, but rather because Jane is too much so.

Emma Woodhouse dislikes Jane Fairfax. And

why? Because, as Emma reflects, 'she could never get acquainted with Jane: she did not know how it was, but there was such coldness and reserve – such apparent indifference.' Jane Fairfax was 'so cautious!' Emma objects, on another occasion. 'There was no getting at her real opinion. She seemed determined to hazard nothing. She was disgustingly, was suspiciously reserved.' And Emma has it in a nutshell: for, Jane Fairfax is so bent on *complete* independence that she is like a kind of fortress, into which no human interest can easily enter and from which little human feeling can be seen to emerge. She has a mind of her own, it is true, and a rather high mind at that, but almost nothing of what is called 'the common touch.' And it will not do in the matter of love; Mr Knightley admits to conversing with Jane Fairfax 'with admiration and pleasure always,' but it is, as he says, 'with no thought beyond.'

Of course, Jane Fairfax too finds a man, ending the novel openly engaged to Mr Frank Churchill. Nevertheless, though Mr Knightley generously predicts that Frank's character 'will improve, and acquire from hers the steadiness and delicacy of principle that it wants,' what he envisages is a union no more desirable than that of Robert Martin and Harriet Smith: while we pitied Harriet for the indignity of having to be raised up by her husband, we need pity Jane no less for the indignity of having to raise her husband up! Neither can look her man in the eye: the one because she must look so far up at him; the other because she must look so far down on him! The Jane Austen woman must not only respect herself much more than Harriet does; she must respect her man much more than Jane does.

The moral of Jane's story, then, is that a woman should not be *too* independent of mind, or she will lack, as Mr Knightley finds Jane Fairfax to lack, 'the open temper which a man would wish for in a wife.'

What, then, of the third and final contestant for the prize of Mr Knightley? What of Emma Woodhouse? Certainly, Emma has none of the excellence of Jane Fairfax's knowledge and accomplishments; she herself understands that the applause she receives for her recital at the pianoforte is mere politeness when compared with the enthusiasm shown for Jane Fairfax's playing. And, in general, Emma has made more lists of books to be read than she has read books. Which is not to say that Emma is *ignorant*, of course; the contrast she makes, not just with Harriet Smith, but with almost all of the novel's characters, reveals her understanding to be strong and her education worthy. 'Mine is an active, busy mind,' Emma tells Harriet 'with a great many independent resources.' And she is right. But she has not mined those resources so completely as Jane has, having been always too engaged with the world and those in it to achieve Jane Fairfax's standard. Anticipating her active old age, Emma says: 'If I draw less, I shall read more; if I give up music, I shall take to carpet-work.' For, Emma is moderately committed to many things, not completely so to anything.

Emma Woodhouse is no Harriet Smith, a mere three sheets in the winds of others' opinions, swaying this way and then that as the weather decides. But neither is Emma another Jane Fairfax, so thoroughly set upon her own course that nothing can redirect her, so high-minded that no one can reach her. 'I have blamed you, and lectured you,' says Mr Knightley, when he confesses to Emma that he loves her, 'and you have borne it as no other woman in England would have borne it.' Certainly as no Harriet and no Jane would have borne it, the former likely to have been obliterated by Mr Knightley's advice, the latter almost certain to have been oblivious to it. Only Emma has just that *moderate* level of independence, which opens her to Mr Knightley's influence without abandoning her to Mr Knightley's will.

But is not this all rather beside the point?, you might ask. After all, modern women require not only a mind of their own but a *life* of their own, not just ideas in their heads but the money in their pockets that comes from equal opportunity and pay. And what, pray, can Jane Austen have to say about this, her heroines, like herself, without much more than a penny to call their own? The entailed estates that so blight the fortunes of the Bennet, Dashwood, and Elliot girls are but grand expressions of what was the general condition of Regency women, who, whatever the extent of their independence of mind, were in total want of independence of means!

And yet, Jane Austen does have something to say on this matter of worldly independence. Rather more, indeed, than we might imagine. Harriet Smith, after all, is not only empty of head, but empty also of pocket, an unfortunate situation that is clearly deplored by her author; how almost impossible!, for a woman as dependent as Harriet is, on the financial support of an anonymous donor, to have anything like the dignity which ought to be her birthright. Jane Austen may have lived at a time when Harriet's situation was not unusual, a time when women for the most part lacked any independence of means, but she had the very great foresight to realize how degrading a condition this could be.

By contrast with Harriet, however, Jane Fairfax seems to want to make herself as independent of means as she is of mind! – the only of Jane Austen's women to even consider such a possibility. And the effect is surprisingly unappealing. Jane Fairfax's pursuit of a career as governess is felt by the novel's characters – and by the novel's readers – to be rather bewilderingly excessive, particularly given her private knowledge that she will never really have to embark on it. But the confusing affair does work to show how exclusive of relationship a woman's focus on material independence can be. Jane Fairfax is presented to us, over and over again, in the act of saying *no* to other people: to Colonel Campbell and his family's protection, to Mrs Elton and her patronage, to Emma and her gifts of fortifying fare, to any company at all on her walks and in her rooms. *No! No! No!* Even her off-stage *Yes!*, to Frank Churchill, before the action of the novel begins, is muffled for almost the entire course of events by her stalwart refusal to disclose their engagement or to show any sign that it exists. She will not, it appears, ask anything of anyone. She will rather, once again, be *completely* independent.

And in this, Jane Fairfax makes a very early warning to every woman since who has pursued independence of means. You see, the duties of love are not doled out in equal measure – when *Persuasion*'s Charles Musgrove shirks attendance on his sick child, on the grounds that, 'Nursing does not belong to a man, it is not his province. A sick child is always the mother's property: her own feelings generally make it so,' our twenty-first-century ears may bridle, but it is almost as true today as it was in Regency times. For reasons biological or cultural, the simple fact remains that it is women to whom fall most of the duties of relationship. And the Jane Fairfaxes of this world are poorly equipped for this fact, so bent on *complete* independence that the duties of relationship can only be felt by them as a burden, a hindrance, an obstacle, a tie. Yet they also, for the most part, continue to carry out these duties – it is still they who take up the responsibilities of cooking, cleaning and general care. With the result that the Jane Fairfaxes of this world – this world's most 'independent' women – are the most shamefully exploited of all, doing a full-time job at 'work' and a full-time job at 'home,' sold on the myth that a woman should be *completely* independent while persisting in bearing out that single simple fact: that it is women to whom fall most of the duties of relationship. We often refer to the Jane Fairfaxes of this world as women who 'have it all'; but they should rather be thought of as woman who take on too much!

Perhaps the first real career to which respectable women had access was the one on which Jane Fairfax seems always about to enter: the career of governess. How fitting!, that this first 'opportunity' for an educated woman to be completely independent of means held before her the prospect that so many careers to which she has since gained access have also held before her: just that miserable combination of the duties of carer and the responsibilities of worker, just that impossible mix of ill-defined and well-defined roles, just that stressful melange of love and of money, that has blighted the lives of women during the last two-hundred years. At one rather fraught point in the novel, Jane Fairfax compares the governess trade with the slave trade – they are 'widely different certainly as to the guilt of those who carry it on,' she says, 'but as to the greater misery of the victims, I do not know where it lies.' And the same might be said of many more modern careers that attract women in pursuit of independence, women on whose rounded shoulders, as on the overworked frame of the Regency governess, very often rest: almost all of the duties of 'home' with almost none of its comforts, and almost all of the duties of 'work' with almost none of its adjournments.

The fact is, the infamous challenge of juggling 'work' and 'home' is now the greatest enemy of women's claim to independence. And we would do well to appreciate that it is an enemy which Regency women were rarely compelled to confront. Not, as one might too quickly conclude, because Regency England simply relegated women to the 'home,' thus precluding them from ever taking 'work,' but because Regency England did not think of 'home' and 'work' in the manner that is now so familiar and so fraught – Forde's draper shop, that bastion of the village of Highbury, was, we can be sure, both work *and* home to the Forde family; behind its counter were to be found both Mr *and* Mrs Forde, no doubt, and any grown Fordes suffered to work and any little Fordes suffered to play. It took the Victorian age, with its crowded cities and filthy factories, to begin to dismantle this set-up, to separate 'home' from 'work,' in a move that has possibly been the single greatest contributor to the plight of Western women ever since, and perhaps the real reason for why the pursuit of independence of means has been, for women, so difficult and self-defeating.

It is no coincidence that all of Jane Austen's heroines marry either a clergyman or a gentleman. For, particularly in the case of clergymen and gentlemen, the homeplace and the workplace were integral, with the clergyman's wife and the gentleman's wife having as much involvement in business as in domestic affairs. And the novel *Emma* – Jane Austen's manifesto for women's independence – takes the point even further than this: when Mr Knightley and Emma marry, not only is Emma set to share with her husband in the gentlemanly duties that will not distinguish between 'home' and 'work,' she is set to do so *on her turf* and not his! In this instance, our knight in shining armour, far from whisking his bride away to *his* great mansion, quietly tethers his trusty steed and moves into *hers*! What a testimony this is!, to the true equality of Emma's relation to Mr Knightley, a mode of relation that does *not* compel the woman to choose as so many women since have had to choose: between 'work' and 'home,' between rights and duties, between life and love.

He 'had never been so bewitched by any woman as he was by her.'

RULE 6

DON'T JUST SIT THERE, *SAY SOMETHING!*

When once you find yourself on a date, the advice of *The Rules* is simply not to talk too much. 'Just listen to what he says,' its authors recommend. 'Follow his lead.' 'Sometimes,' they continue, 'men just want to drive in silence without saying a word. Let them. Maybe he's thinking about how he's going to propose to you one day. Don't ruin his concentration.' And, for the *girl* whose chief concern is to *capture* her man, this might just do it!

But for the Jane Austen woman, the idea of sitting demurely in the passenger seat while the man of whom she is supposed to be an equal occupies the driving seat, not just of the car but of the conversation, is, frankly, offensive! The advice that we remain silent, just in case our man is composing his proposal, implies that, by speaking, we would inevitably diminish his enthusiasm for doing so – it implies, in short, that women, like Victorian children, are creatures better seen than they are heard. But the Jane Austen woman is not a child – *she* does not just sit there, with her man in the driving seat, but *says something*, and does it rather well!

Of all of Jane Austen's heroines, it is, perhaps, Elizabeth Bennet who is the best instructor in this matter. Full of wit and with a love of repartee, in the course of the novel she succeeds almost literally in talking Mr Darcy to life!

On one of the first occasions on which Elizabeth and Darcy are in company together, Elizabeth's mother, a woman herself bursting with conversation (though it is usually more eager than it is interesting!), ill-advisedly holds forth on an early love affair of Jane's. It ended without engagement, Mrs Bennet admits, but she proudly informs her listeners that the gentleman in question did write some very pretty verses. 'And so ended his affection,' Elizabeth interrupts, impatient to call a halt to her mother's mortifying efforts to impress Mr Bingley with Jane's powers of attraction.

'I wonder,' she continues, 'who first discovered the efficacy of poetry in driving away love!'

With one short but pithy interjection, Elizabeth not only derails her mother's chatter, but calls the company's attention away from the subject altogether by airing an opinion entirely the opposite of a generally accepted one. Mr Darcy cannot resist the challenge.

'I have been used to consider poetry as the *food* of love,' he responds.

And Elizabeth's next stroke is one of genius.

'Of a fine, stout, healthy love it may. Everything nourishes what is strong already. But if it be only a slight, thin sort of inclination, I am convinced that one good sonnet will starve it entirely away.'

We are told that 'Darcy only smiled.' But we can infer that he has already begun to feel intrigued by one whose conversation is as animating as her countenance is attractive.

What are *we* to learn from this short exchange? A very great deal, if we wish to. For one thing, we might immediately notice that Elizabeth is not confined to anybody's passenger seat!, but takes it upon herself rather to direct the course of proceedings than anything else. And this is done with charm and originality, the key to which is the irresistible playfulness of her manner. 'I have had the pleasure of your acquaintance long enough,' Mr Darcy says to Elizabeth later in the novel, 'to know that you find great enjoyment in occasionally professing opinions which in fact are not your own.' Mr Darcy has observed Elizabeth well. Whether or not she *really* considers poetry to be the driver-away of love is indeed uncertain: the effect of her interjection lies not in its truthfulness but in the mischievousness with which she expresses and then defends an opinion that is out of the ordinary, and therefore easy for the company to respond to if they will. Perhaps, after all, poetry is the food of love, and perhaps, on serious consideration, Elizabeth really believes so. But, had she interrupted her mother with

'And so ended his affection. Which is surprising, given that poetry is generally thought to be the food of love,'

she may have succeeded in distracting Mrs Bennet from making any further embarrassing communications, but it is doubtful whether anything else would have occurred more than a round of nodded assents and, perhaps, a few half-hearted 'Indeed's. Mr Darcy may still have smiled, but it is certain to have been a rather thin and polite smile, and equally certain that he would have forgotten Elizabeth's conversation the moment he heard it, and likely forgotten Elizabeth too!

When Elizabeth finds herself an unexpected guest at Netherfield Hall, during an illness that has confined Jane to one of the rooms there, Miss Bingley, one evening after dinner and when Elizabeth has excused herself from the company, begins abusing her to those gathered round, observing of Elizabeth's manners that they are 'very bad indeed, a mixture,' so Miss Bingley describes it, 'of pride and impertinence.' As well as having no style and no beauty, Miss Bingley declares, Elizabeth has also 'no conversation.' Once again: Poor Miss Bingley! *She* is perhaps one of those women who might be better served in love were she to remain silent when she has the urge to speak; her conversation appears to consist of little more than a clichéd contempt for the countryside and catty criticisms of her rival. But Elizabeth, precisely because of the playfulness that Miss Bingley mistakes for impertinent pride, is a Jane Austen woman through and through, for whom silent acquiescence would seem a degrading road to love.

The word was a pejorative one in Jane Austen's time, and applied rather to Lydia Bennet's reckless pursuit of officers than to any more sophisticated interaction with the opposite sex; but in our vocabulary today, there is no better word to describe Elizabeth's playful conversational style than – *flirtation*. And flirtation is an art that we ought all to attempt to add to our list of accomplishments.

That flirtation *is* an art, and an important one at that, is shown most forcibly by those who have no talent for it. Take our poor Miss Bingley, a woman of whom it might certainly be said that her aim is to *capture* the heart of Mr Darcy. One evening, again during Elizabeth's stay at Netherfield, Miss Bingley takes to walking about the drawing room with the object of trying the effect of her elegant figure and graceful movement on a rather indifferent Fitzwilliam. At last, and in some desperation, she invites Elizabeth to join her, thus succeeding in her object of causing Mr Darcy to look up from his book. Immediately, Miss Bingley invites him to add to their little party. He declines, on the grounds that they can have only two objects in walking about the room together and that he would be in their way in either case. 'What could he mean?' Miss Bingley wonders aloud. And when he explains, with a degree of flirtatious fun of his own, Elizabeth's advice to Miss Bingley on how to proceed with him is very simple: 'Tease him – laugh at him.'

But Miss Bingley, of course, cannot do it. 'Tease calmness of manner and presence of mind!' she objects. 'Laugh without a subject! No, no!' Elizabeth, for her part, feels no such compunction and, in playful tones but with serious intent, with that 'mixture of archness and sweetness' that Mr Darcy cannot resist, suggests to him that his faults might include vanity and pride, and that he shows very great signs of a propensity to hate everybody! Has she gone too far? Not a whit! Mr Darcy, after all, owns much of the county of Derbyshire and is regarded by the world at large as a man to be universally desired – a woman must take very great care if she is not to be, as Miss Bingley so clearly is, overwhelmed by his wealth and position. And indeed, though only a very few men command Mr Darcy's level of influence, in the main it still is a man's world, and we women must take often drastic measures to ensure we do not find ourselves overawed. The best way to do this is, as Elizabeth says, to tease our man, to laugh at him, to *flirt* with him.

'Just listen to what he says,' the authors of *The Rules* advise us. 'Follow his lead.' But nothing could be further from the Jane Austen woman's mind. And, strange though it may seem, there is a scene in *Pride and Prejudice* exactly calculated to prove that *The Rules* has got it wrong! We are at Netherfield Hall, once again, on the occasion of Mr Bingley's ball. Mr Darcy, almost against his will, has asked Elizabeth to dance, and they stand now, face to face in the line of couples. If ever there was a ritual designed to remind us that a woman should remain in the passenger seat, to be taken where her man chooses to go, it is the one that is about to begin! The musicians strike their first chord, Mr Darcy offers his hand, and Elizabeth, along with every other woman in the line-up, begins to *follow his lead* ...

But, true to form, and in spirited defiance of the age-old tradition in which she is taking part, Elizabeth steals the show. Though she is led by Darcy through the dance moves, it is he who is led by her through the conversational moves. Having made a slight observation on the ball, to which he replies only briefly, she draws herself up to her full height and, far from leaving him to his silence, rather commands:

'It is *your* turn to say something now, Mr Darcy. I talked about the dance, and *you* ought to make some sort of remark on the size of the room, or the number of couples.'

Once again, we are told that Mr Darcy smiled; how could he not, in the face of such mischievous defiance! This is small talk made by playing with small talk; and, all of a sudden, small talk no longer seems so small. When Mr Darcy assures Elizabeth that he is ready to say whatever she judges necessary to be said, she answers:

'Very well. That reply will do for the present. Perhaps by and by I may observe that private balls are much pleasanter than public ones. But *now* we may be silent.'

It is a master class. Asked to dance by a man in respect of whom all the world would advise her not to talk too much but to *follow his lead*; going through learned-off motions that are nothing less than a ritual reminder that men lead and women follow: Elizabeth takes charge of the conversation with such expert assurance that Mr Darcy cannot but submit. *Follow his lead*? Rather say, lead *him* a merry, playful, flirtatious dance, and see whether he is able to follow you! Mr Darcy, in the end, finds that he cannot help but follow Elizabeth, rather as one under a very agreeable spell. We are told that he 'had never been so bewitched by any woman as he was by her.'

Perhaps, however, some of us are about to shut up this volume with a sigh, and with the thought that, empowering as it might be to live one's life as a Jane Austen woman, it is an option not open to us all.

Elizabeth Bennet may indeed be bewitching, but she cannot be an example to those of us who are naturally quieter, naturally serious, and who shudder at the prospect of those verbal battles into which Lizzy enters with such energy and expertise. It may be that, were we to emulate Elizabeth's style, we would be found as attractive a prospect as Mr Darcy evidently finds her, but we some of us simply cannot do it!

But all is not lost. It is true, Elizabeth is Jane Austen's showpiece in the matter of conversation, but hers is not the only style of which Jane Austen approves. Consider *Persuasion*'s Anne Elliot: though perfectly good humoured, she is, on the whole, a serious person, even a grave person, for whom the sparkling repartee of an Elizabeth Bennet would be utterly out of character. Nevertheless, Anne Elliot is not *silent*, waiting patiently in the passenger seat while Captain Wentworth carries the day with his gregarious personality. On the contrary, Anne conducts many conversations throughout *Persuasion*; it is just that they often take place to stage left or right of the main action, so to speak, while the drivers and the passengers play their roles on centre stage.

Take the occasion at Lyme, on the night before Louisa's fateful fall, when we are told that Captains Harville and Wentworth led the conversation in one part of the room: Anne finds herself in discussion with James Benwick, the melancholy young sailor who has recently lost his wife. With him, she considers the merits of various leading poets of the day, and the nature of those who enjoy poetry most, and the importance of including a greater allowance of prose in one's literary diet. Benwick is a serious man, who has had all the advantage of education and experience. But Anne is more than equal to their exchange; far from simply listening to what Benwick has to say, she feels in herself 'the right of seniority of mind' and recommends to Benwick authors from whose writing she judges he might take consolation.

And then, of course, there is that momentous conversation between Anne and Captain Harville, played out at one of the windows in Mrs Musgrove's room in Bath, with Captain Wentworth engaged in writing a letter of business close by. The topic is the relative fidelity of men and women, and it is discussed with such a degree of seriousness and feeling that Captain Wentworth, who cannot help himself from listening in, at one time drops from his hand the pen with which he is supposed to be writing. At the climax of the exchange, Captain Harville moves to defend his claim for men's greater constancy, by making an appeal to literature.

'I do not think I ever opened a book in my life,' he says, 'which had not something to say upon woman's inconstancy. Songs and proverbs, all talk of woman's fickleness.'

But Anne will not follow his lead!

'If you please,' she objects, 'no reference to examples in books. Men have had every advantage of us in telling their own story. Education has been theirs in so much higher a degree; the pen has been in their hands. I will not allow books to prove anything.'

Anne Elliot may be quiet, gentle and serious-minded, but she is no silent passenger in this conversation! And she concludes it in a style so eloquent and a tone of such conviction that it is no wonder Captain Wentworth is at that very moment composing a hasty letter in which he confesses that she is piercing his soul!

'I believe you equal,' says Anne to Captain Harville, 'to every important exertion, and to every domestic forbearance, so long as – if I may be allowed the expression – so long as you have an object. I mean while the woman you love lives, and lives for you. All the privilege I claim for my own sex (it is not a very enviable one; you need not covet it), is that of loving longest, when existence or when hope is gone.'

Captain Wentworth, we are told, 'can listen no longer in silence.' He is 'every instance hearing something which overpowers' him. Right then and there, with the pen and paper that are at hand, he offers himself to Anne once again, 'with a heart even more your own than when you almost broke it, eight years and a half ago.'

The Rules says: 'Sometimes men just want to drive in silence without saying a word. Let them. Maybe he's thinking about how he's going to propose to you one day. Don't ruin his concentration.' *The Jane Austen Rules* says: 'Speak up! Make him unable any longer to listen in silence! Upset his concentration! Rob him of the ability to continue with his thoughts and his tasks! Overpower him, so that he feels a strong urge to propose to you *right now*!'

On a first date, *The Rules'* rule is to be seen but not heard, so that your Mr Right will 'think you're interesting and mysterious.' On a first date, and on all dates, *The Jane Austen Rules'* rule is to be seen *and heard*, so your Mr Right will *know* that you're interesting and mysterious, and bewitching and overpowering, and all *because of*, not in spite of, what you say!

The significance of an eyebrow raised or an
eyelid lowered can be analysed for hours . . .

RULE 7

NO GIRLFRIENDS

Even *The Rules* acknowledges that sitting demurely in the passenger seat, while saying almost nothing, is more than a little unnatural. Which is not to say that its authors take pity on us and retract their advice – but they do concede to us a *safety valve*, to offset the frustrations of an evening spent being seen but rarely heard. 'Wait until the date is over,' they say, 'and then you can call ten girlfriends and analyse the date for hours.' But we should beware even of *one* 'girlfriend,' never mind the ten *The Rules* would apportion us! For the truth of the matter is that 'girlfriends' are the enemies of love. Why this? Because 'girlfriends' work to syphon off those thoughts and feelings about our relationship, which ought, albeit more moderately, to be confided in our man. If the first Jane Austen rule is to be a woman not a girl, then the seventh Jane Austen rule is to have women friends not girlfriends!

It is to *Sense and Sensibility* that we must turn at this juncture, a novel which revolves around the very important question of how much to confide, and to whom, of our romantic relations. At its centre is a love triangle, formed by Edward Ferrars, Elinor Dashwood and Lucy Steele. And she who emerges victorious is *not* she who does the Regency equivalent of calling ten girlfriends and analysing the date for hours! On the contrary, the victor is Elinor Dashwood, who, despite being sorely tried by circumstances, resists the dubious comfort of girlfriends and rationally regulates her relationship talk.

Elinor Dashwood has very good women friends, in her mother and her sister, but she is remarkable for her stoical refusal to transform her women friends into those cavernous repositories of romantic thoughts and feelings that are what we call 'girlfriends.' In love, from early in the novel, with the very worthy Edward, Elinor keeps command of her thoughts and feelings until Edward, at last, declares that he returns them. Upon this happy occasion, Elinor's dramatic outburst – rushing from the room in tears of joy – reveals what has been her exemplary control, over thoughts and feelings that are quite as strong as we would expect those of a woman in love to be. This is not to say that Elinor has been a fraud, pretending to an indifference towards Edward that she does not feel – at one point, upon being quizzed by Marianne on the topic, Elinor confides, calmly and honestly, that she thinks highly of Edward, that she esteems him, that she likes him. But, when compared with the effusions that are currency between girlfriends, such rational talk seems pale and rather uninteresting. Marianne, for one, is disgusted: 'Esteem him!' she taunts. 'Like him! Cold-hearted Elinor! Use those words again, and I will leave the room this moment!'

The great irony of *Sense and Sensibility*, however, is that Elinor is *made into* a girlfriend, and by the very woman whose secret betrothal is the cause of Elinor's romantic miseries! Lucy Steele, to whom Edward became engaged during an early and enervating tuition by Lucy's uncle, we are told misses no opportunity of engaging Elinor in conversation, 'or of striving to improve their acquaintance by an easy and frank communication of her sentiments.' And so Elinor becomes the girlfriend of Edward's fiancée, forced to endure the miseries of this ill-advised female relation while availing herself of none of its dubious advantages. 'Your secret is safe with me,' Elinor promises, upon Lucy's demand that her newly made girlfriend tell nobody what has just been told to her so very openly. 'But pardon me,' Elinor continues, 'if I express some surprise at so unnecessary a communication.' Elinor may resist the urge to relieve herself of Lucy's confidence by making girlfriends in her turn of her mother and sister – she does not reveal Lucy's secret even to Marianne – but she cannot resist the urge to point out to Lucy how absurd it really is for a woman to unburden her heart of what ought to be shared with her man.

Lucy Steele, by her own admission, has not seen Edward Ferrars on more than eight occasions during their four-year engagement. But, in spite of protestations of suffering (which Elinor, like us, does not believe), she appears to be coping rather more than tolerably. And that, in short, is the trouble with girlfriends: they undermine the relevance of your man! After all, what need is there for contact with your boyfriend when you have girlfriends to service the emotional side of life?

It is a very curious development: the shift in Lucy Steele's affections at the close of *Sense and Sensibility*, from Edward Ferrars to his younger brother Robert. Less curious than it might have been, it is true, had Edward not been recently disinherited. But even this does not quite account for the suddenness with which Lucy falls out of love with a man to whom she has been engaged for four whole years, and of whom she, not more than a few weeks before, had been speaking to Elinor in phrases of ardent devotion. But that is just it! The fact that Lucy was in the habit of speaking *of* Edward means that she was not in the habit, nor much desirous, of speaking *to* Edward. Consequently, Edward's substitution is effected with much less pain than one might have predicted. It is easier to replace a minor actor than it is to replace a leading man; and girlfriends make minor actors of our leading men! What is the difference between an Edward and a Robert, when much of the romance of relationship is played out with our girlfriends and not our boyfriend!

And there is worse – girlfriends are the enemies of love in an even more sinister sense. The great temptation to indulge in what is called 'girl-talk' is the pleasurable prospect of almost endless speculation on what are often rather minor occurrences: the significance of an eyebrow raised or an eyelid lowered can be analysed for hours, after which eyebrows and eyelids have acquired a kind of world-historical importance! Of course, no actual eyebrow, no real eyelid, is ever *that* important. And so, girlfriends would much rather that eyebrows and eyelids not be around very much, to upset the dramatic effect. Girl-talk is so much easier when its subject is not present to put a stay upon it. A boyfriend, in other words, is only ever inconveniently real!

Which gives us fulsome explanation for Lucy Steel's abandonment of Edward: it is not, after all, on account of his loss of realty, but on account instead of his wealth of *reality*! Edward, a secret fiancé never on the scene, is one, rather exciting, thing; Edward, an ordinary parson never off the scene, is another, rather too stubbornly real, thing! Once they are free to be together, Lucy can hardly contain her desire to be apart. She reports in a letter to Elinor, that during the first 'two happy hours' they spent in each other's company in many years, she earnestly recommended to Edward that they go their separate ways and 'would have parted forever on the spot, would he consent to it.' Edward, Lucy says, would not consent to it, and so she is shortly driven to parting forever on the spot without his consent, exchanging the domestic and loyal Edward for his younger brother, Robert, a man much more of the fashionable world and therefore much less likely to discommode a fiancée and wife by the disappointing reality of his presence!

For her part, Elinor is rewarded for a novel's worth of discretion by a relationship in which the 'easy and frank communication of sentiments' that Lucy Steele indulges in with her girlfriends occurs, as it ought to do, within the relationship and not without. For Elinor, the physical presence of Edward, far from being inconvenient, is an absolute necessity. Upon their engagement, we are told that Edward remained at Barton Cottage for a whole week, on the grounds that nothing less than a week could suffice 'to say half that was to be said of the past, the present, and the future.' Jane Austen continues: 'For though a very few hours spent in the hard labour of incessant talking will despatch more subjects than can really be in common between any two rational creatures, yet with lovers it is different. Between *them* no subject is finished, no communication is even made, til it has been made at least twenty times over.' So, you see: left to its own devices, love *will* give us the opportunity for hours of analysis of the details of its unfolding, which we are taught to think is possible only with girlfriends. What a blessing it is!, that Elinor did not spend her romantic communications in the hyperbolic hot-house known as 'girl-talk,' but reserved them for the person who knows how to value them most: the man who is, after all, their object.

Miss Caroline Bingley, one evening at Netherfield Hall, remarks on 'those young ladies who seek to recommend themselves to the other sex by undervaluing their own.' Miss Bingley correctly observes that it is a 'paltry device.' But it is not the only trick to which young ladies are wont to resort. For, there is that other paltry device, practiced by young ladies like Lucy Steele, who seek to *relieve* themselves of the other sex by *over*valuing their own! Between these devices, of undervaluing other women and overvaluing other women, there is, of course, the very recommendable resort of, simply, *valuing* other women! – of rationally and maturely availing ourselves of female friendship. Jane Austen, of all authors, knew how very important it is that we cleave to the worthiest women around us. Her heroines are remarkable for their all of them having at least one female friend as comfort and counsel: Elizabeth has her Jane; Emma, her Mrs Weston; Anne, her Lady Russell; Catherine, her Miss Tilney; Elinor, her Marianne; and Fanny, at last, her sister Susan.

Three of these heroines, it is true, for a time undergo the evils of being without such a friend: Catherine Moreland, just embarking on society, is in very great danger of making a girlfriend of Isabella Thorpe until she is rescued from the mistake, by her own good sense and by the advent of estimable Miss Tilney. And Fanny Price, at the mercy of those whose society Sir Thomas chooses to cultivate, is driven to the limits of her faculties to resist the inferior intimacy offered by Mary Crawford. Not until her own sister, Susan, is grown up and taken to live at Mansfield, does Fanny put down her guard and allow herself the advantage of female friendship. Worst of all, however, is Marianne Dashwood, who, though well provided with the society of admirable women, delays availing herself of their friendship until it is almost too late for her to profit from it.

How different Marianne's tale from that of Elinor! – the younger sister so irrationally secretive about her affair with Mr Willoughby that even she, in the end, cannot tell what's going on! Are they engaged or are they not?, is the burning question of much of the novel, and Marianne herself appears confused, having never taken the opportunity to gain that clarity and perspective that a sympathetic ear and sensible advice, particularly of Elinor, would have furnished. For, if girlfriends would heighten the significance of boyfriends to an extent that sets reality at nought, then women friends tend to have that very opposite effect: of tempering our tendency to exaggerate in love with a very healthy dose of what is true. And Marianne, like many of us, is sadly in need of this effect, having, from the outset, far too developed a wont to idealise the merits of her man. Before she has even met him, she describes to her mother how he will 'enter into all of my feelings'; and once she has met him, she is so immediately convinced of their being kindred spirits that she declares seven hours to have been sufficient for their knowing each other absolutely! It is a sad journey for Marianne, from this hyperbole of enthusiasm to the tragic truth that Willoughby is a scoundrel, but it is a journey she might have spared herself had she made friends of the women who surround her.

Marianne comes close to death in the process of learning this lesson. But there really is no need for any of us to do the same, when all we have to do is to follow the Jane Austen rule: hold close to your women friends, but *no girlfriends* if you please!

*It is not enough to see, but to consider what
you see; not enough to look at goings-on,
but to observe goings-on.*

RULE 8

PROVE IT

Important as are your women friends, there is, in the end, only one person who can decide on the merits of your man: *you*. After all, if it were a case of murder and not of love – if death really had come to Pemberley! – the testimony of your women friends, be they ever so reliable, would count for nothing more than hearsay; only you can give the eye-witness evidence to justify that elusive final verdict. Then, to solve the mystery of love, make very very sure you look for proof!

But is not this a rather grisly rule for love? Is not the task of searching for clues rather too sordid to be in any manner romantic? What of simply listening to your heart? Trusting to your instincts? Going with your gut? An investigator may get closer to the *facts* of your relationship, but will she ever get closer to the *truth* of it? Does not love require something far more intuitive than a simple weighing up of the evidence? To be sure, it does! But then, so does all detective work. As anyone will know who likes the odd 'who-dunnit?,' a good detective does always begin with a hunch. Only by proving this hunch, however, can a mystery ever be unravelled. Listen to your heart, then, by all means. But do not omit to look at all the facts!

And be aware – looking at all the facts requires something quite deliberate and calculating. It is not enough to see, but to *consider* what you see; not enough to look at goings-on, but to *observe* goings-on. An eye-witness uses more than just her eyes; she makes very good use of her head too. All of which may seem quite out of place in a *love* story, of course. But, then, what of that? Love stories are full of tragic endings! Far better take a leaf from the detective story, and secure for ourselves a happy ever after.

Anne Elliot is perhaps Jane Austen's worst romantic heroine, being rather too quiet and cautious to fit easily into the role. But she is certainly Jane Austen's best romantic detective. At the age of nineteen, she was persuaded to reject a good man on what were rather shaky grounds. At the age of twenty-seven, however, she will not be persuaded to anything else – not, that is, without sufficient proof. Lady Russell, her esteemed and loyal friend, wishes Anne to accept the advances of charming Mr Elliot. But Anne knows now what she did not know eight years earlier: that her own eye-witness account is far more convincing than even Lady Russell's mere hearsay contribution. 'Lady Russell,' we are told 'saw either less or more than her young friend, for she saw nothing in Mr Elliot to excite her distrust.'

But it is quite clear that Lady Russell saw *less* – for Anne combines a privileged first-hand experience with an admirable capacity to analyse that experience, making her testimony against Mr Elliot quite simply conclusive. It is worth quoting it here at some length, as its fine detail and careful deliberation are, in this matter, exemplary:

'That he was a sensible man, an agreeable man, that he talked well, professed good opinions, seemed to judge properly and as a man of principle, this was all clear enough. He certainly knew what was right, nor could she fix on any one article of moral duty evidently transgressed; but yet she would have been afraid to answer for his conduct. She distrusted the past, if not the present. The names which occasionally dropt of former associates, the allusions to former practices and pursuits, suggested suspicions not favourable of what he had been. She saw that there had been bad habits; that Sunday travelling had been a common thing; that there had been a period of his life (and probably not a short one) when he had been, at least, careless in all serious matters; and, though he might now think very differently, who could answer for the true sentiments of a clever, cautious man, grown old enough to appreciate a fair character? How could it ever be ascertained that his mind was truly cleansed?'

There is nothing romantic in this, Anne Elliot's prosecution of her cousin, merely a cool and calm assessment of the facts. But a cool and calm assessment of the facts is the very thing required when you're in love! We do not, after all, wish to commit the gross injustice of finding the wrong man guilty, or of allowing the guilty man to walk free!

This is precisely the injustice described in the pages of *Pride and Prejudice*, in which Elizabeth Bennet, generally a super-sleuth of human nature, listens to her heart but does *not* look at the facts. Jane Austen initially intended this novel to be entitled 'First Impressions,' because it is, in the end, an entertaining lesson, in the danger of simply trusting to your instincts, of forming first impressions but never having second thoughts!

Elizabeth first meets George Wickham on a street in the local village of Meryton. It is a fine morning, but her walk to Meryton has been sullied, by the company of two silly sisters and one odious cousin. And then, as if heaven had sent him, there appears before her a handsome young soldier, whose manners and bearing are more than a match for his looks. What an addition, to an otherwise unremarkable militia! What an arrival, to an otherwise unremarkable town!

Elizabeth, sharp-witted as she is, is quick to form a pretty robust hunch in Wickham's favour. And very natural and appropriate that she should! – so long, of course, as she then sets out to prove it. And nothing ought to have been easier. For, the evidence begins to mount almost at once, on that very evening in fact, at a card party in Meryton, when Mr Wickham, unprompted, discloses to Elizabeth the intimate details of his history with the family of Darcy. But Elizabeth has ceased to play detective, at the very moment when it would have served her most: neglecting to observe how odd it is that a man she barely knows should confide in her so completely, she notices nothing but Wickham's handsome looks and Wickham's tragic tale. A more unreliable witness could hardly be conjured! – Wickham even goes so far as later to drop Elizabeth for a Miss King with ten thousand pounds, and still Lizzy finds him innocent, arguing that 'handsome men must have something to live on as well as the plain.' Here is a lesson indeed: our naturally penetrating observer of humanity, unable to see what is before her very eyes!

Thankfully, what is before her very eyes is finally presented to Elizabeth in such a way as to make it impossible for her not to observe it. Mr Darcy, offended by Elizabeth's peremptory rejection of his marriage proposal, is moved to write a long letter, in which he provides all the necessary evidence of his family's dealings with Mr Wickham. 'This must be false!' Elizabeth exclaims, upon perusal of Darcy's testimony. 'This cannot be!' – her hunch about Mr Wickham is slow to lose its hold. Not for long more, however, as Elizabeth, at last!, begins to take the case to a review. Wickham's early confidences *now* appear as utterly indelicate; Wickham's avoidance of the Netherfield ball, utterly inconsistent; Wickham's defamation of the Darcy name, utterly unscrupulous; Wickham's pursuit of Miss King, utterly mercenary; and Wickham's attentions to herself, utterly gratuitous. As for her own blindness, her own refusal to look at all the facts, this now appears to Elizabeth as utterly humiliating! She reflects on how little she had inquired about Wickham's 'real character,' on how 'his countenance, voice, and manner had established him at once in the possession of every virtue,' on how, in short, she had trusted so much to her hunch that she had forgotten to bother to prove it.

Towards the close of *Pride and Prejudice*, Elizabeth observes of Mr Wickham and Mr Darcy, that 'one has got all the goodness, and the other all the appearance of it.' In murder-mystery terms, we might simply say that Mr Darcy *looks guilty*! But looks do not suffice to build a case on. In the end, only the facts can be admitted. And the facts, it turns out, are all in Darcy's favour. With the result that, in the case of *Wickham v. Darcy*, Lizzy must come to a verdict exactly the opposite of her first suspicions. Mr Darcy is found innocent of all charges, and set free into a happy ever after, while Wickham is judged guilty by unanimous decision and transported to a lifetime's labour in Newcastle!

Pride and Prejudice, like all the best detective stories, incorporates what is a killer twist, a turn of events so dramatic that nothing any longer looks the same. The character who seemed most innocent becomes the chief suspect; the one who had looked most guilty is found to have been unable to commit the crime. And in these circumstances, Elizabeth, like all the best detectives, shows herself to be as willing to alter her opinions as she had been apt to form them – we would judge her harshly, would we not, were she to stick to her early suspicions once the new and dramatic evidence has comes to light?

And yet, when it comes to love stories, we often expect her to do just that, to remain constant and un-wavering – under the silly but common misconception that love, if it is true, must never change. In the Oscar-winning screen adaptation of *Sense and Sensibility*, Kate Winslet's Marianne – a character pain-fully in need of some good detective work – stands atop a rainy hill, gazes down at the future residence of Mr Willoughby, and whispers to herself in abject misery the immortal words of Shakespeare himself: 'Love is not love, which alters when it alteration finds ... Oh no! It is an ever fixed mark that looks on tempests and is never shaken ... and bears it out, even to the edge of doom.' But Jane Austen, in this matter at least, talks infinitely better sense than William Shakespeare, when she tells us that love may very well have to change its mind, that love may very well even have to die!

And what is more – we know it. After all, were Elizabeth, upon opening her eyes to the true nature of Mr Wickham, to continue in love with him on the principle that love bears it out even to the edge of doom (in this case, even as far as penury in Newcastle), we would find her as ridiculous as we would find Miss Marple, were she to stay with her suspicion that the butler did it, when all the evidence had begun to point to the maid! Because, in the end, we are really well aware that love ought very seriously to consider altering when it alteration finds, and that love ought not to be too fixed a mark, and that love ought to look upon tempests with a rather wary eye, and that love ought to have no intention whatsoever of getting anywhere near the edge of doom! For, true love is love that has stood the test, not just of time, but of thought. True love is love that has been *proven*.

But after all of this detective work, perhaps it will be no harm to end on a sweeter note. Then, here it is: when Elinor Dashwood first meets Edward Ferrars, everything she subsequently discovers about him corroborates her first instincts; when Jane Bennet takes a fancy to Mr Bingley, everything he says and does thereafter adds to the force of her initial conviction; when Fanny Price, at the tender age of nine, decides on the worth of Edmund Bertram, nothing ever occurs to sway her from it; and when, after eight long years, Captain Wentworth and Anne Elliot come together once again, their first impressions of each other have, in all that time, done nothing else but tally with the facts. We may find, you see, that our hunch is proven right – that love at first sight was true love after all!

Not enough conversation had together
to feel rooted in mutual understanding.

RULE 9

DON'T JUST SIT THERE,
DO SOMETHING!

Imagine, if you will, that you have been given the gift of a young plant, say one of those climbing roses that make such a pretty picture against the walls of English cottages. It comes to you straight from the nursery, already with a bud or two, a promise of great splendour to come. Delighted with your gift, you sit for some time admiring it and imagining in what corner of your garden it will look best. And then ... *nothing*! No transplanting, to stretch those roots for feeding. No training, to support those tendrils for growing. No watering, to plump those buds for flowering. The most promising young plant in all the world could not withstand such neglect. This one withers in its pot, its first flower dead before it opens ...

And now, imagine, if you will, that you have, at last, found true love. The relationship you have longed for is granted to you, and you sit back for some time, in the warm glow of budding love. And then ... nothing! Or, at any rate, *not enough*. Not enough time spent together to support each other's needs. Not enough meals taken together to nourish growing affection. Not enough conversation had together to feel rooted in mutual understanding. The most promising young love in all the world could not withstand such neglect, except as a rather withered version of what it might have been. Meeting Mr Right is all very well, but it counts for little if you do not *tend* your relationship with him. Hence the ninth *Jane Austen* rule: when once you have found true love, don't just sit there ... *do something!*

It is true, of course, that Jane Austen's novels are full to the brim with couples who do a great deal of sitting there and doing nothing for their relationship! *Pride and Prejudice*'s Mr Bennet spends hours on end sitting there in his study, into which no-one, including his wife, is usually granted admittance. Sir Thomas Bertram is absent for a chunk of the novel *Mansfield Park*, and, even when at home, is rarely in company with a wife who does little more than sit there on the sofa. And, in a general way, the husbands and wives of Jane Austen's fiction are so *divided*, by the shooting of pheasants and the sketching of flowers, by the playing of cards and the netting of purses, by the drinking of port and the taking of tea, that Mr and Mrs Collins's rather frosty mode of relationship might be taken to define almost all of the unions described by the pen of Jane Austen: Mr Collins, sitting there in his book room, looking out of the window onto the road; and Charlotte, sitting there in her back room, chosen specifically for its being unlikely to tempt Mr Collins to abandon his own quarters and spend some time with her!

The wonder is that the marriages described by Jane Austen manage to survive at all! Why has Mr Bennet remained so many years with a wife with whom he feels so little sympathy? Why has Sir Thomas not long since forsaken the limp and laudanum-soaked Lady Bertram? The reason, of course, has to do with *climate*: Regency England's was far more favourable to relationships than our own, the institution of marriage being at its very core. Indeed, we might go so far as to say that a budding relationship in Regency England could *hardly but* take root and flourish, so rich was the soil and sturdy the trellis that custom provided for its sustenance. What would now be taken as the merest hint of a green shoot of love was, in those days, taken as a fully developed declaration of intent, which activated traditions of a force we can hardly imagine, so that those involved, even if they did nothing at all for their relationship, were bolstered by a very sturdy precedent. Long-established rules of courtship were set in train, the inevitable engagement was relatively short, and the subsequent marriage conducted according to conventions so unquestionable as to nourish even couples as incompatible as Mr and Mrs Bennet, or Sir Thomas and Lady Bertram.

And this kind of matrimonial support may, indeed, have had its advantages. But Jane Austen is far from commending to us the many relationships that would, without it, have been unable to prop themselves up. For Jane Austen knew, with all of that insight beyond her time and place on account of which she is still read and admired today, that a relationship cannot bloom as it ought to bloom unless it is carefully tended by the two people in it. Oh, the Mr and Mrs Bennets shambled along together in a sort of way, but Jane Austen saw that the mere rote formality of their relationship was as unsatisfactory a version of true relationship as an artificial plant is of the much-loved English rose.

But there is a great difficulty about the ninth Jane Austen rule – a difficulty which caused Jane Austen to have to illustrate it mostly by *counter* example, by the Mr and Mrs Bennets and their like. And the difficulty is this: doing something for and with one another, tending our relationship, involves just that everyday, slowly accumulating, unheralded kind of activity that lacks precisely the drama and excitement that we turn to novels to provide us with! Jane Austen must run the risk of writing an undramatic novel, if she is to try teach us the ninth Jane Austen rule! And yet she felt compelled to teach us the ninth Jane Austen rule, because doing something for and with one another, tending our relationship, involves just that everyday, slowly accumulating, unheralded kind of activity that we are in greatest need of being encouraged to!

This was true even in Jane Austen's time, but how much more true it is in ours. For, we are wont, nowadays, to demand of life all of the drama that used to be demanded only of novels. We twenty-first century creatures *tire* so – of the job we do, of the house we own, of the person we love, of our clothes, our hair, our hobbies, and live in a kind of feverish state, constantly bombarded by communications that work rather to separate us than to bring us together. Take the modern-day couple, 'doing something together' on a Saturday afternoon, sitting side-by-side on the couch perhaps … each with a screen before their eyes! Modern day Mr and Mrs Collinses, in other words, who might as well be sitting in opposite-facing rooms for all the *true* togetherness their greater proximity implies. The plastic 'fern' in the corner of the room is not more unsatisfactory a version of its living breathing counterpart than is this modern couple of a real relationship.

Let us pause for a moment, then, to honour Jane Austen, who risked her very reputation as a novelist for the sake of teaching us to do something for love – she used her last-completed novel to describe just that everyday, slowly accumulating, unheralded kind of activity whose *un*dramatic effect might have caused *Persuasion* to fall, unread, into the dustbin of literary history! It is certainly a quieter novel that all the rest, with a more serious, even a sombre, tone. Its heroine is more mature than any other, and graver, almost melancholy sometimes. And its starring relationship is, crucially, the longest lived, eight whole years having passed since Anne Elliot and Captain Wentworth first became engaged: with *Persuasion*, Jane Austen comes as close as she dares to depicting a relationship that is past its first flush of love. And all in order to persuade us that a truly happy ending involves not just finding a man, but, having found him, doing so much for and with him that our relationship grows into the kind of sturdy tree that gives us shade in sun and shelter from rain, and that throws out enough broad, low-lying branches for ourselves and our children to climb upon and lean against.

Persuasion is a novel in which the theme of doing something for love is so central that it comes up for discussion between the novel's characters. The scene is the Great House at Uppercross, and around the Musgroves' dinner table is gathered the usual company, including Mrs Croft, Captain Wentworth's only sister. Talk turns naturally to naval matters, and Captain Wentworth holds forth with a piece of uncharacteristic false gallantry: he hates, he claims, to see women on board ship, and will not, if he can help it, ever admit such a circumstance on any vessel of his. What nonsense!, objects his sister immediately. 'Women may be as comfortable on board, as in the best house in England.' Mrs Croft is a woman who has done so much for love that she has, for its sake, even gone to sea!: in the fifteen years of her marriage, she reports, she has crossed the Atlantic four times, been once to the East Indies and back again, as well to Cork, Lisbon and Gibraltar. And the only time she ever felt unwell, she tells the company gathered around the Musgroves' dinner table, was during a winter that she spent by herself in Deal. 'I lived in perpetual fright at that time,' she says, 'from not knowing what to do with myself.' And so Mrs Croft ought to have lived in perpetual fright; for, sitting there on dry land and not doing something for your relationship is a perilous practice indeed!

There is little doubt that Anne Elliot will *not* make such a mistake – hers is a nature that must always be doing something for those around her. At the very opening of the novel, when her father and older sister are forced to address the crisis to which the family finances have come, it is Anne and only Anne by whom the option of active economy and busy retrenchment is preferred; Sir Walter and Elizabeth, lazy and self-indulgent, choose the far less onerous path of simply removing themselves to a smaller establishment in Bath. Upon this removal, it is Anne who remains behind, to catalogue the books and pictures, to arrange the distribution of plants, to visit every house in the parish, and a thousand other tasks that nobody not attuned to such activity could ever acknowledge or appreciate. 'Dear me!' says her sister, Mary, when Anne excuses her delay in visiting on account of all she has had to accomplish at Kellynch, 'what can you possibly have to do?' And yet, Mary has summoned Anne to Uppercross to do precisely what she has been doing at Kellynch: all of those small domestic chores that are noticeable by most only when they are not attended to.

When Louisa Musgrove finally falls from the Cobb at Lyme, and everybody seems as if paralysed by inaction, Anne's readiness for action might seem somewhat out of character. But it is really only a public performance of what has, throughout the novel, been her unseen, and mostly unacknowledged, wont to be doing something for others. As Captain Wentworth so feelingly remarks, upon his recommending Anne as the best possible nurse for Louisa: 'no one so proper, so capable as Anne'!

So much for *Persuasion*'s leading lady; *she* is well-practiced at doing something for others and can certainly be relied upon to do something for love. Anne, we are told in the novel's very last sentence, 'gloried in being a sailor's wife,' and will do no less than Mrs Croft, it is clear, in exerting herself for the good of her relationship. But it is not only women who must do something for love – men must do something too, for all that they are far-too-often excused from this responsibility! What, then, of *Persuasion*'s leading *man*? Captain Wentworth is a sailor, of course, one to whom doing something for King and Country is, no doubt, second nature. But what of doing something for love? Is Captain Wentworth capable of that? Not only capable, is Jane Austen's reply, but eminently capable, the very last part of the novel's very last sentence reserved for recommending the naval profession, as being 'if possible more distinguished in its domestic virtues than in its national importance.'

Take Captain Harville, Captain Wentworth's good friend, whose wife is so determined to do something for love that she overcomes even Captain Wentworth's disinclination to have women on board ship, insisting upon being carried by him from Portsmouth to Plymouth to keep her husband company. The Harvilles are remarkable for the manner in which, with the smallest possible income, they have fashioned a home and a life between them. During a visit to their lodgings at Lyme, Anne is struck by the 'ingenious contrivances and nice arrangements' that have transformed what would otherwise have been cramped and sparsely furnished quarters. Captain and Mrs Harville are a couple who have clearly done something for and with each other every minute of every day of their married lives, Mrs Harville taking to the life of a sailor with enthusiasm and ease, and her Captain, now wounded and unable to go to sea, 'with constant employment within. He drew,' we are told, 'he varnished, he carpentered, he glued;

he made toys for the children; he fashioned new netting-needles and pins with improvements; and if everything else was done, sat down to his large fishing net at one corner of the room.' Even when he is sitting there, Captain Harville is doing something for love!, and, upon quitting the house, Anne thinks to herself that 'she left great happiness behind her.'

But there is, for Anne, great happiness also *before* her, as Jane Austen reveals with a very simple scene, giving the reader a satisfying premonition of the manner in which Anne and Captain Wentworth will eventually conduct their married life. It is a short scene, too lacking in incident, we might think, to be of much significance; but it is one of the occasions on which Jane Austen dares to depict that everyday, slowly accumulating, unheralded kind of activity that makes relationships thrive but novels potentially dull ...

Little Charles Musgrove, having recently fallen from a tree, is lying on the sofa in the parlour of Uppercross Cottage. His aunt Anne is kneeling by his side, attending quietly to his wants and needs. Also in the room are two who are waiting for others in the house to appear: Charles Hayter, a cousin; and Captain Wentworth. The door is opened from without, and Anne's youngest nephew, a boy of about two, makes his way into the room. There being nothing much to attract his attention, this small boy does as all small boys might do: he begins to climb on the back of kneeling Aunt Anne, his little arms fastened tightly about her neck and his little mind made up on never ever being shaken off again! Anne entreats, cajoles, orders and admonishes, but all in vain. Then Charles Hayter, with the right of an older family member, intervenes: 'Walter,' he says, 'why do you not do as you are bid? Do not you hear your aunt speak? Come to me, Walter, come to cousin Charles.' But still, our bold little Walter does not stir; and Anne's head is bent down so much by his weight that she can no longer look up from the floor; when, without a word of warning, she is suddenly released. Walter's hands are unclasped from around her neck and he is resolutely borne away. Where all of cousin Hayter's words are in vain, a simple, silent action wins the day. As we are told: 'Captain Wentworth *had done it*'!

Say it with flowers, one hears so often these days. Say it with chocolates, say it with a card, say it with a kiss ... It seems, indeed, that we have forgotten the insignificance of saying it, when compared with the effectiveness of doing it! Talk is cheap, as the old adage would have it. And it is. Oh, we may dream romantic dreams, of those moments when love is professed and sweet nothings are whispered in our ear, but, if we do, we ought to recall what is still one of the most romantic moments in the whole of English literature, when Anne Elliot, exhausted from a long walk in the country but politely declining the Crofts' offer of a seat in their carriage, is obliged by Captain Wentworth to be assisted into the gig – not by any *words* of concern, nor by any *statement* of affection, but 'quietly,' with his strong arms for her support. He had seen her fatigue and resolved, 'without a word,' to give her rest. Is there a reader in all the world whose fibres have not thrilled to realize, with Anne, that 'his hands *had done it*'!

The sixth *Jane Austen* rule is: Don't just sit there, *say something*! Contrary to the advice of those who recommend that we sit quietly in the passenger seat while our man commands the wheel, Jane Austen would have us teasingly hazard a comment, flirtatiously open a topic, seriously talk on a subject of mutual interest. But we are now further along on the road of love, and an even greater effort is required of us: the effort of *doing*, not merely of saying.

And Admiral and Mrs Croft, into whose conveyance Captain Wentworth's hands silently deliver his exhausted Miss Anne, show us, once again, how it is done. The Admiral is in the driving seat, it is true, but so often does Mrs Croft contribute to their progress, by alerting the Admiral to an obstacle or by placing her hand on the reins to avoid a ditch, that the whole effect is of a curricle driven by *two*. It is an effect that Anne imagines to be 'no bad representation of the general guidance of their affairs.' And it is an effect that Jane Austen holds to be no bad model for the general guidance of *ours*. Mrs Croft, far from sitting silently in the Admiral's passenger seat, not only *says something* but *does something* too! And so, indeed, must we.

First comes love, then comes marriage,
then comes baby in a carriage.

HAVE *GREAT*
EXPECTATIONS

Elizabeth and Darcy
Sitting in a tree
K-I-S-S-I-N-G
First comes love
Then comes marriage
Then comes baby
In a carriage.

That, as they say, is how the story goes. And it's no good, our feigning surprise! After all, one cannot open a book like *The Jane Austen Rules* and still claim never to have in mind such a story. Indeed, most of us have it so much in mind that we must force ourselves to read through the opening lines, without our thoughts too often straying to the closing ones! – how many times have we found ourselves getting ready for a first date, as yet even to begin k-i-s-s-i-n-g!, and all the while wondering whether it would be more convenient to live together in his part of the city or in ours? The old hobby of writing our name with his surname on a piece of paper is, perhaps, a rather childish one, but, if we are honest, we will admit to having done a version of that very thing, not just once but every time we think we have found the right man. And why not? What is the point of pretending never to have heard the old story of love? *First comes love, then comes marriage, then comes baby in a carriage*: it's such a classic tale, even a child could repeat it!

Which makes it all the more astonishing that, when once established in a relationship, when once in a situation in which we might really begin to expect the old story of love to proceed in the usual way, so many of us begin to act as if we have never been told it! When anything arises relating to marriage and children, we adopt a wide-eyed attitude, as if the whole story is *news to us,* as if *we* have *no expectations*. But Jane Austen would have us put a stop to such nonsense this instant! Have great expectations!, is her advice. Anything less is not only disingenuous, it is downright dangerous too.

The most frustrating set of events to arise in Jane Austen's fiction occurs in the novel *Sense and Sensibility.* Very early on, Elinor Dashwood meets and falls in love with the brother of her own brother's wife. Edward Ferrars is likeable, rich, and clearly as enamoured of Elinor as she is of him. It is a perfect beginning, and we wait for their story to unfold, secure in the knowledge of what is to come. There is some concern, of course, over Edward's family, but he has shown himself to be so independent of worldly approval that we, like Elinor, feel pretty certain that even the prospect of disinheritance will not prevent him from acting according to his own judgment of what is right and good. Like Elinor, we greet his every appearance on the page as the promise of a declaration of affection. Like Elinor, we glance impatiently ahead a few chapters to see how long more we must wait before Edward determines to speak. But nothing happens! The story refuses to unfold as we, like Elinor, expect: Edward remains silent, the Dashwoods go to Devon, and nobody at all lives happily ever after.

All, of course, is soon revealed. Edward, very simply, has a prior engagement, having proposed marriage to a young Miss Lucy Steele some four years before our novel begins. That is why he does not propose to Elinor, that is why their story does not meet our expectations ... and that is the point at which our frustration turns to confusion!

Edward's prior engagement is a twist in the tale and no mistake. But it is not fatal, surely! It is not the end of the line, surely! He and Lucy, by his own eventual admission, were betrothed at a particularly dull period in Edward's life, when he was in sore want of company and consolation. But he is not to be bound by this betrothal, surely! He is not to be held continually to a promise made in error, surely! Let him explain the matter to Lucy, and, whether or not she accepts his explanation, let him sever the ties between them. It is not as if Lucy is the type to die of a broken heart. She is, as Edward realised too late and as Elinor describes it to herself, 'illiterate, art-ful, and selfish,' a woman for whom only Edward's position in the world is of any consequence. Edward does not have to marry Lucy ... *SURELY!*

But Edward does have to marry Lucy ... and surely! It is one of the very striking things about the whole affair: Lucy Steele's *assuredness* throughout. Even Elinor remarks upon it, observing somewhat slyly to Lucy that, had the strength of her and Ed-ward's attachment to each other failed, as it would have between many people under similar circum-stances, her situation would have been 'pitiable indeed.' Lucy, however, is not to be discomposed. 'Edward's love for me,' she calmly replies, 'has been pretty well put to the test, by our long, very long ab-sence since we were first engaged, and it has stood the trial so well, that I should be unpardonable to doubt it now. I can safely say that he has never gave me one moment's alarm on that account from the first.' But this is too much to be borne! Is Lucy Steele *inhuman*, to have no doubt, no niggling uncertainty, that Edward and she will see through the story of love, marriage, and children, in spite of hardly seeing each other during four whole years? As readers, we must admit to being flummoxed! Does Lucy Steele know something that we do not?

Well yes, she does. For, not only does Lucy Steele know, as we all know, that *first comes love, then comes marriage, then comes baby in a carriage*, Lucy Steele also knows that it serves a woman very badly not to have great expectations that this story will be her story too. She and Edward fell in love, albeit four years ago. She and Edward even declared their love and became engaged, albeit four years ago. And so, she and Edward are now as honour-bound to marry each other as they would be were they walking up the aisle together as we speak! In other words, Lucy Steele knows that the fact that Edward is not *actually* married to her is almost beside the point: every week that has passed during which they have *not* turned their thoughts to anyone else, every ball they have gone to at which they have *not* stood up with anyone else, every letter they have written and every lock of hair they have bestowed, has implied again and again that the old story of love, marriage, and children will, for them, run its usual course. And with the nerves of steel that her name suggests are hers, Lucy is not about to deny that she has *every* expectation it will do just that!

Jane Austen carries this point so far as to meet Lucy's great expectations, of becoming, in the end, Edward's lawfully married wife ... for a whole half-chapter at any rate!, during which all that we and Elinor know is that Lucy Steele has changed her name to Ferrars. The fact that it turns out that Lucy has married Edward's brother and not Edward himself is, of course, necessary to the happy ending of the novel, but Jane Austen hopes that that half-chapter will have done its work, to drive home the rule that, when one has put time and effort into a relationship, one has the right to great expectations that everything else will follow suit. Although we, like Elinor, flinch at the news of Lucy's marriage to Edward, Jane Austen will tolerate no indulgence on our part in any sense of grievance at the development. Marianne, who has still much to learn of love, may fall back in her chair in hysterics, but we, like Elinor, must content ourselves with going pale, and sit stoically in the knowledge that nothing has occurred that we, along with Lucy and all right-thinking people, did not expect.

But what of Elinor?, we might object. Lucy Steele may have been within her rights to her great expectations of Edward Ferrars, but what of Elinor's expectations, raised very reasonably by Edward's behaviour towards her during his early visit to Norland Park, before anything was known of his secret betrothal? Is it only when we are actually engaged that we have the right to great expectations? Does the story really read like this: *first comes ENGAGEMENT, then comes marriage, then comes baby in a carriage*? Does Jane Austen have no support to offer those of us who merely *love*, those of us who have spent time and effort for the sake of a relationship but have not engaged to take things any further?

Fear not – Jane Austen is the champion of us all, whether we have a ring on our finger or not. Edward stayed on with the Dashwoods at Norland Park during week after week, paying Elinor every attention and growing quite obviously more attached to her every day that passed, and Jane Austen leaves us in no doubt that, for this reason, Elinor had as much right as Lucy had, to her great expectations of him. It is a grave fault in Edward that he permitted himself to give rise to them, and Elinor tells him so herself: 'Your behaviour was certainly very wrong,' she says, when they are, at last, united. 'To say nothing of my own conviction,' she continues, 'our relations were all led away by it to fancy and expect what, as you were then situated, could never be.'

Elinor's scolding is naturally not very harsh, but the point has nonetheless been made: everybody has the right to great expectations that their love story will unfold in the usual manner; and nobody has the right to behave in such a way as to raise those expectations if they are unable or unwilling to fulfil them. If you have devoted time and effort to a relationship, you should have as bright a prospect of getting married and having children as someone who has become *engaged* to do so. Indeed, becoming engaged to do so usually does nothing more than make explicit what has been implicit for quite some time. It is for this reason that engagements are rarely greeted with any surprise, either by the people who get engaged or by the family and friends to whom the engagement is subsequently announced. For, engagement or no engagement: *first comes love, then comes marriage, then comes baby in a carriage!*

We will, therefore, now know how to value Captain Wentworth's sense of his responsibilities, when, just at that moment in *Persuasion* when he admits to himself the strength of his feelings for Anne Elliot, he discovers from his friend Captain Harville that his behaviour towards Louisa Musgrove during the past few months has given rise to great expectations, among her family and perhaps even in herself, that he intends to marry her. No sooner, as he reports in the end to Anne, had he 'begun to feel himself alive again, than he had begun to feel himself, though alive, not at liberty.'

It is heart-breaking, of course. With Anne picking her way between the puddles of Bath, we are desperate for Captain Wentworth's reappearance on the scene. Where *is* he?, we wonder, our patience running thin. But he is exactly where he ought to be: if not quite by Louisa's side (he is human, after all!), then waiting on the wings ready to commit to her as fully as he has, albeit somewhat unwittingly, given her reason to expect he will. Captain Wentworth is not engaged to Louisa Musgrove. And yet, as he explains to Anne, 'I was no longer at my own disposal. I was hers in honour if she wished it'!

But *now* we may think that Jane Austen is too enthusiastically our champion!, too fervent in demanding that the very slightest occasion be allowed to warrant the very greatest expectations! How will it all end, we may wonder? Will men be afraid even to raise a smile, lest in doing so they raise our expectations? Will men cease so much as to glance in our direction? At this rate, meeting a man will be all but impossible!, with every good specimen in virtual hiding, hands clasped firmly behind their backs and eyes fixed determinedly on a neutral point in the middle distance! This won't do! - the claims of Lucy Steele we might be persuaded to support, but the claims of Louisa Musgrove? All that happened was a little mild flirtation! Are great expectations to arise even from that? We won't have it! We will not argue the case of a foolish young girl, who is smiled at by a good-looking man and expects him to walk down the aisle with her as a consequence!

But we ought to pause a moment to consider Jane Austen's position. In Regency England, it was often the case that even a very young woman, if apparently jilted in love, would either lose her bloom and fade from the social scene into the life of an old maid, or be considered in some manner culpable, 'damaged goods' as it were, and not, therefore, to be taken up by anyone else. For this reason, though *we* might judge the grounds for Louisa Musgrove's great expectations to be rather shaky, it is perfectly right that Captain Wentworth should consider them solid indeed: he has been so unguarded in his behaviour as to give the impression of fancying Louisa, and his was a time in which even faint impressions in this matter were more or less tantamount to fervid intentions.

Ours is, of course, a very different time, in which

matters of the heart have not the urgency they had for Louisa Musgrove, in which a woman has much more time at her disposal then the likes of Louisa enjoyed. And yet, even modern life is, as the saying goes, short! Even modern women do not have an infinite amount of time! But you wouldn't know it by observing us: years spent trying out one relationship and then another; and, when we eventually meet the right man, years spent ... well, in *love*, presumably, but with apparently no expectations that *then comes marriage, then comes baby in a carriage*!

Indeed, the having of no expectations is all but a mantra for modern womanhood, the thing above all others that shows how far we have come, how liberated we have been. We adopt an attitude of non-committal carelessness: we are 'not looking for anything'; we have 'no agenda'. And we justify this attitude by juxtaposing it with what we claim to despise: the iron rod of the Lucy Steele variety, beating her man into shape; and the limp figure of the Louisa Musgrove variety, clinging helplessly to her man as if he were a rock. We determine to ourselves to be neither strong-armed woman nor weak-willed girl; we resolve neither to dictate the life of another nor to be taken by the hand and dictated to ourselves.

But the problem with 'liberated' women is that, by focusing always on being neither *steely* nor *needy*, we fall again and again between these two options! Neither hard enough nor soft enough, neither Lucy enough nor Louisa enough, we end up expecting neither our demands to be answered nor our desires to be met, almost as if living with a man because we have expectations of marriage and children is as despicable as visiting an invalid because we have expectations of an inheritance! But these are very different kinds of expectation: if one is monstrous and petty; the other is natural and *great*.

Perhaps, in the end, we need simply to ask ourselves this: why, after two hundred years, do we still enjoy Jane Austen's novels? The answer, you see, is quite straightforward: Jane Austen's novels do, all of them, tell us that well-worn, time-honoured *story of love*. Their author adds twists and turns to its progress, of course; she puts obstacles in its way and places hurdles in its path. But she leaves it, after all, to follow its usual course:

> Elizabeth and Darcy
> Sitting in a tree
> K-I-S-S-I-N-G
> First comes love
> Then comes marriage
> Then comes baby
> In a carriage!

Reader, I married him.

READER, *MARRY HIM*!

'Reader, I married him' is not a line to which Jane Austen has any recourse, but the reason for this pertains to *style*, not to *substance*. All of Jane Austen's heroines, do, in the end, *marry him*; indeed, hers is as rousing a campaign in favour of matrimony as, perhaps, has ever been launched!

And yet the modern reader may not be so easily convinced that there is much merit in getting married. In fact, the modern reader may see getting married as just about the worst thing she could do! Why? Because the modern reader is likely to be aware that, for most of its history, marriage has been a tawdry transaction, a convenient way of transferring property (including women!) from one man or set of men to another. Marriage has been the marketplace in which female flesh has been sold to the highest bidder, the guarantee that women had no means and no rights. No *name* even, the convention still to this day being to refer to a woman as *Mrs Fitzwilliam Darcy*. As if Elizabeth Bennet had never existed!

And there is no denying it: the modern reader has a point. Marriage has all too often been no friend to women. But the question follows: *what then*? Must we begin all over again, right from the start? Must we find an alternative, not just to marriage but to everything that has, at one time or another, undermined women's claim to a status equal to men? And consider: this turns out to mean ... well, *everything*! The world has been so consistently unfriendly to women that, were we to reject all that has oppressed us, we would, it is to be feared, have very little left!

Take books, for example. Not only have books been written almost exclusively by men, they have, for the most part, actively broadcast the idea that women are the inferior sex. 'I do not think I ever opened a book in my life,' says Captain Harville to Anne Elliot, 'which had not something to say upon woman's inconstancy.' And Anne's short reply says it all: 'Men have had every advantage of us in telling their own story. The pen has been in their hands.' But the question still follows: *what then*? Are we to boycott all books because they have, in the main, been prejudiced against us? Are we to remain illiterate? Anne Elliot does not think so, being more than equal to conversing with Captain Benwick on the subject of books, and recommending to him a variety of titles from which she believes he will benefit. Anne does not deny herself the very great pleasure of reading just because books, like everything else, have not been a friend to her sex.

And we must feel very glad that Jane Austen

agreed with her! True, books were, in one sense, no friend of Jane Austen. She even had to conceal her identity in order to publish them, submitting her novels as having been written by 'A Lady,' so that her readers would take them to be merely demure sketches of country life rather than the incisive handbooks on human nature that we now understand them to be. But what Jane Austen knew is what Anne Elliot knew: that it is often wise to work to change things from within rather than start all over again, without.

Reader, there are some things we humans have done for a very, very long time. Reading and writing books is one of them. Getting married is another – it is, we might say, a classic institution. But if so, it is like all classics: not simply old but good, not simply enduring but worth enduring, not simply historical but modern too.

Why does Catherine become the wife of Henry Tilney? Why does Marianne wed her Colonel Brandon? Why does Elinor walk down the aisle with Edward? Why does Emma give her hand to Mr Knightley? Why does Elizabeth exchange those vows with Darcy? Why does Fanny say 'I do' to her Edmund? Why does Anne take Captain Wentworth til death do them part? The answer to all of these questions is quite simple: getting married is still the best way we know of getting closure – in novels *and in life*! And, for all our modern talk of keeping our options open, closure, in the end, is what we like – in novels *and in life*! Then, Reader, follow the Elizabeths, the Catherines, and the Elinors; Reader, *marry him*!

The Elizabeths and the Catherines and the Elinors are all very well, you might say – but what of the *Janes*? Why did Jane Austen not get married? Are *we* to tread the path down which *she* would not venture? But Jane Austen *did* venture down that path, and the story is worth the telling:

It is November 1802. Jane and her sister Cassandra are staying at their old home at Steventon, now occupied by their brother James and his family. From there, they travel to nearby Manydown, to stay with their friends, the Bigg-Withers. Only a day or two later, however, early on a Friday morning, a distraught Jane and Cassandra arrive back at their brother's door, demanding to be taken immediately from the neighbourhood, and back to their new home in Bath. For, it turns out that twenty-one-year-old Harris Bigg-Wither proposed to his sisters' lively and pretty friend, Jane, only the evening before. And what is more, *Jane said yes*! It is just that, early this morning, she changed her mind and said no!

In Harris Bigg-Wither, Jane Austen may, for all we know, have found true love. His sisters were her dearest friends, he had an excellent character, fortune and position, and he was six years younger into the bargain! And any remaining doubt on the matter must be put to rest by the fact that Jane Austen decided to marry him! True, she decided *not* to marry him very shortly afterwards, but recall that, in Regency England, freedom was in so short a supply that one had to stand guard fiercely over the very little of it one had at one's disposal. Jane Austen, living with her parents and sister in Bath, was free to pursue her writing; Jane Bigg-Wither, mother of a young family and in charge of a household, would not be, not because we know Harris Bigg-Wither to have been a despotic man but because those were the times they lived in: a single woman had little enough freedom; a married woman almost none.

Then, Reader, instead of thinking that Jane Austen did not marry so why should we, rather think: Jane Austen did not marry so that we *should* marry, with all the advantages of having entered into marriage on the terms of *The Jane Austen Rules*. She worked hard within one classic form – the book – so that we might take advantage of another classic form – marriage. Having said no to Harris Bigg-Wither, she returned home to write a series of novels whose advice on love would prove a matrimonial game-changer, for the women of her time and, yes, for the women of ours.

Reader, consider how glad we all feel, when Elizabeth and Darcy say 'I do'! How merry, when Anne and Captain Wentworth exchange their vows! How heartened, when Catherine marries Henry, and how pleased, when Elinor marries Edward! Then why not feel glad and merry and heartened and pleased at *ourselves*, as we sign up for better and for worse with a man who is worthy of it all? There will be no cause for worry as we do so, no reason for an inkling of concern, for we will have met this man and dated this man and at last agreed to marry this man according to rules that take from marriage all that might be bad and leave to marriage all that will be good. We will have met this man and dated this man and at last agreed to marry this man, in short, by *The Jane Austen Rules*.

Our current enthusiasm for screen adaptations of Jane Austen claims again and again to have found a 'modern take' on the classic. But it is no less important to find a classic take on the modern. Hence *The Jane Austen Rules* – a classic guide to modern love.

ABOUT THE AUTHOR

Sinéad Murphy teaches philosophy at Newcastle University. She is the author of *Effective History: On Critical Practice Under Historical Conditions* and *The Art Kettle*.